THE
LIGHT TOUCH
COOKBOOK

OTHER BOOKS BY MARIE SIMMONS

Fresh & Fast

Lighter, Quicker, Better (with Richard Sax)

Muffins A to Z

Bar Cookies A to Z

Italian Light Cooking

Rice, the Amazing Grain

365 Ways to Cook Pasta

The Bartender's Guide to Alcohol-free Drinks

THE
LIGHT TOUCH
COOKBOOK

All-Time Favorite Recipes Made
Healthful & Delicious

MARIE SIMMONS

Illustrations by Barbara Maslen

CHAPTERS™

CHAPTERS PUBLISHING LTD., SHELBURNE, VERMONT 05482

Published by
Chapters Publishing Ltd.
2085 Shelburne Road
Shelburne, VT 05482

Library of Congress Cataloging-in-Publication Data

Simmons, Marie
The light touch cookbook : all-time favorite recipes made healthful & delicious /
by Marie Simmons; illustrations by Barbara Maslen.
    p.   cm.
Previously published: 1992
Includes index.
ISBN 1-57630-023-4
1. Low-fat diet—Recipes. 2. Cookery, American. I. Title.
RM237.7.S57 1996
641.5'638—dc20   96-26767

Printed and bound in Canada by
Best Book Manufacturers, Inc.

Designed by Susan McClellan

Cover illustration by Barbara Maslen

ACKNOWLEDGMENTS

With very special thanks to:

Tamara Holt, a smart cook
Rux Martin, a terrific editor
and
Gretchen Semuskie, my conscientious recipe tester

Contents

INTRODUCTION

It's a very odd thing—
As odd as can be—
That whatever Miss T. eats
Turns into Miss T.
                    —Walter de la Mare

THIS LITTLE POEM is taped to my refrigerator. In my opinion, it is both more frivolous and more effective than most warnings to midnight snackers. As I swing her past my face and out of sight, the unseeing Miss T. encourages me to grab a carrot, not a wedge of Cheddar. Instead of facing down one of those bossy red STOP! signs I've seen on other people's refrigerators, I enjoy imagining Miss T.—or me—turning into either a sad blob of heavy mayonnaise or a crisp, healthy stick of celery.

In a less literal way, I've come to believe that we really are what we eat—that eating well is one sure route to a true feeling of well-being, if not to good health and longevity as well. My American-born Italian mother was an accomplished cook who knew, apparently by instinct, that a balanced diet, one that included vegetables, grains, meats, poultry, pasta and seafood, was the way to eat. Sweets were only for special occasions, and dessert was always fruit. I can still hear her no-nonsense voice proclaiming, "I would rather spend my money on good food than on the doctor."

Now, years later, my mother can point triumphantly to the daily news items reporting on "her" findings. Some of the most compelling support for the way my family ate—and the vital link between diet and health—comes from the now-famous Seven Countries Study done in the 1950s. It uncovered a startling difference in the eating habits of men who suffered from heart problems and those who did not. Finnish men, who ate foods rich in saturated (animal) fat, had a high incidence of heart problems, while Greek men, who used mostly olive oil rather than animal fat, had fewer difficulties.

While nutrition studies come and go, this one remains tantalizingly intact, with an increasing number of current scientific research supporting the conclusion that we should eat less fat of all kinds and emulate a diet similar to that of the Mediterranean, with lots of complex carbohydrates—dried beans, rice, pasta and other grains—and an abundance of fruits and vegetables.

UNFORTUNATELY, THE SOCIETY in which we live does not encourage the smartest nutritional habits, with a diet fueled by abundant, inexpensive supplies of butters, creams, oils, eggs and well-fattened meats. In the face of all the scientific evidence against doing so, most of us still eat a diet that derives 42 percent of calories from fat instead of the recommended 30 percent or less, probably because we can't figure out how to fix our fat-laden specialties and don't want to give them up.

Before I began to see the wisdom of Miss T., I fell into a few fatty traps of my own, developing a yen for deep-fried potatoes and Eggplant Parmesan, with its thick slices of eggplant fried in oil and layered with gooey mozzarella. A dense, made-from-scratch chocolate pudding had become my midnight ally, and paté-rich meat loaf with chicken livers and heavy cream had turned into standard fare for Saturday night suppers and sandwiches throughout the week. Clearly, some serious scrutiny was in order.

Without becoming phobic about food or trying the usually ineffective route of total deprivation, I set out to apply my natural tendency to play with recipes in a moderate, cool-headed approach to reducing their fat. Looking for a few quick successes, I began with obvious, popular recipes that seemed amenable to improvement. From experience, I knew that simply leaving out the fat without compensating for its omission was not a satisfactory solution: the results were bound to be bland.

Instead of deep-frying French fries, I tossed them with a little oil and "fried" them on a cookie sheet in a hot oven. To add a jolt of flavor without salt, I sprinkled over some finely chopped fresh garlic and herbs. I brushed a robust-flavored extra-virgin olive oil on eggplant slices and relied on the heat of the oven to brown them. With unsweetened cocoa powder and low-fat milk, I made a surprisingly rich chocolate pudding. I even transformed our beloved but fat-riddled meat loaf, adding lentils and vegetables and lacing it with fresh ginger and soy sauce, so that my family cried not for mercy but for seconds.

SOON I WAS EXAMINING the ingredients and methods of all our good old standby recipes and coming up with a list of alternatives. Was it possible to use a leaner cut of meat? If so, would this cut require a different cooking method to keep it just as tasty? Should I add herbs, the rich, meaty taste of sautéed mushrooms or slowly cooked onions? Would a hot oven brown better than a skillet? Could I use broth instead of oil to cook the vegetables? Could I add more aromatic vegetables? Make a sauce from pureed vegetables? Add more potatoes? More vegetables? Add lemon zest or lemon juice to brighten the flavors? Use a nonstick skillet? As I worked, I asked: Can I simplify the technique so the food tastes every bit as good?

Slowly, I developed a repertoire of flavors and techniques that I almost unconsciously began to integrate into my cooking. Influenced by my heritage, I turned to the robust taste of olive oil, the tanginess of grated Parmigiano-Reggiano or Pecorino Romano cheese, the deep, rich flavor of roasted vegetables (especially garlic and red peppers) and the subtle highlights of fresh herbs: rosemary, parsley, oregano and thyme. The instinct to use more of a gusty ingredient to achieve flavor without tipping the balance of a recipe is undoubtedly something I acquired by birth as well as by experience.

Particularly in low-fat cooking, though, practice and trial-and-error are essential. I learned that it is impossible to reduce fat in some recipes without its loss being apparent. Simply substituting low-fat cheese and milk for the usual Cheddar and whole milk left my Macaroni & Cheese wan-tasting, and introducing sun-dried tomatoes or cottage cheese didn't help. Some recipes are better off left alone. In such cases, I prefer to eat the real thing less often than to feel cheated by a low-fat imposter.

WHILE STREAMLINING my recipes, I constantly penciled notes in the margins on successful strategies, products and flavors, as well as nutritional information. These are preserved as "Tips" found next to the recipes in this book and can be used to apply my techniques to your own favorites.

The Light Touch Cookbook is as much about good eating as it is about reduced-fat cooking. It is not a low-calorie or "diet" cookbook. Like Miss T., it tries to deliver its message with a broad streak of common sense and without the heavy hand that is so often found in "low-fat" cookbooks. Throughout, I have concentrated my energies on adding good flavor rather than on merely taking away fat. At its heart, my philosophy, like my mother's, is all about simplicity, quality and good taste.

A Note on the Nutritional Analysis of Recipes

THE RECIPES IN THIS BOOK were analyzed by Karen Brasel, using the Nutritionist III computer program, *Pennington's Food Values of Portions Commonly Used* and *Agriculture Handbook No. 8.*

The following guidelines were used in determining the analysis:

✳ When a recipe offers a choice within the ingredient list (e.g. "1 cup yogurt or low-fat milk"), the first ingredient listed is the one represented in the recipe analysis.

✳ When an ingredient is listed as "optional," it is not included in the analysis.

✳ Ingredients added "to taste" are not included in the analysis.

✳ When a range of serving sizes is given, the recipe is analyzed for the larger portion of food: If it "Serves 4 to 6," it is analyzed for 4 servings.

A Dozen Points of Light

Reducing Fat Without Sacrifice

✳ Use heavy pans with good-quality nonstick coating. To preserve their nonstick surface, use plastic or wooden spoons, never metal.

✳ Use vegetable-oil cooking spray to coat pans when cooking meat.

✳ Reduce the oil used to sauté chopped onions and other vegetables in traditional recipes by one-half to one-third. Use low heat when cooking so the vegetables' natural moisture can be coaxed out into the pan. If preferred, add a tablespoon of water or broth to the oil.

✳ Whenever possible, replace butter (a saturated fat) with monounsaturated olive or canola oil.

✳ When preparing pasta, save some of the cooking liquid and use it, instead of oil, to moisten the noodles.

✳ Remove the skin from chicken breasts, thighs and legs before cooking.

✳ Steam rather than sauté vegetables.

✳ Replace cream with whole milk, yogurt, low-fat ricotta or cottage cheese; substitute egg white for whole egg. Replace whole milk with low-fat or skim milk.

✳ Use egg white instead of whole egg when coating fish or meats with crumbs.

✳ Look for reduced-fat cheeses in the market.

✳ Use combinations of vegetables and grains instead of meat as a main dish.

✳ Steam, braise and broil without adding fat. Reduce the amount of fat normally used when roasting.

Chapter 1

BREAKFASTS &
BEVERAGES

BREAKFASTS & BEVERAGES

As a child, I was a finicky eater, but I loved breakfast. Most mornings, my mother would serve me a soup bowl filled with oatmeal, to which I would add a lump of butter, a pool of heavy cream and a sprinkling of sugar. I remember slowly stirring it all together and watching in fascination as the pool of cream became tiny streams and the butter mysteriously melted away. Then, as Mom nodded in approval, I devoured every gooey mouthful.

Mom's basic instinct was right. Nutritionists agree: Eating breakfast is important. Or, as a diet-consultant friend observes, "Skipping breakfast and overloading at lunch is like driving 300 miles on an empty tank of gas and then filling up at the end of the journey."

In reality, though, an estimated 30 percent of the population does just that, skipping breakfast altogether. If they grab a bite on the run, it's often a doughnut made with white flour deep-fried in fat and dredged in sugar. When they sit down to a more leisurely feast, one aspect of the meal still doesn't improve: the proverbial plate of fried eggs, bacon and lavishly buttered toast gets fully half its calories from fat.

Even inherently healthful breakfasts like oatmeal can turn into an orgy of fat and cholesterol after the cream and lumps of butter have been added.

The good news is that it is possible to eat—and enjoy—traditional breakfast foods like omelets, pancakes, cereals, muffins and thick slices of toasted bread and still keep a handle on fat calories. For instance, a slice of whole-grain bread slathered with reduced-fat ricotta or cottage cheese and jam provides as much energy as the same slice covered with butter, but with far less fat. Whole-grain cereal with fresh fruit in low-fat milk is every bit as tasty as sugar-coated cereal in half-and-half. Using vegetable oil and fruit produces muffins as tender as those made with butter or margarine, and an omelet with half as many whole eggs plus beaten egg whites is a deliciously light alternative to the traditional whole-egg omelet—with half the fat and cholesterol.

By applying subtle strategies like these, the following recipes offer wholesome, nourishing breakfasts that any mother could love—all with a little less fat.

WESTERN-STYLE FLUFFY OMELET

Makes 2 servings

* *Bacon and cured meats that are bright pink in color most likely contain nitrates and nitrites. Read labels carefully to check for their presence, eat these meats in moderation or seek out brands that do not contain these substances.*

* *In the realm of cheeses, real Cheddar is among the most fat-dense. There are several sensible alternatives:*

■ *Eat less of the real thing. Cheese can be "extended" by coarsely shredding and sprinkling or melting it over your favorite dish. One tablespoon of coarsely shredded cheese is only about ½ ounce.*

■ *Avoid nibbling on "chunks" of cheese. This habit quickly adds up to ounces and double-digit fat grams.*

THE "WESTERN OMELET" at the diner where I worked weekends while in high school was a popular breakfast for the farmers in the region. Softly scrambled eggs were wrapped around a savory filling of minced onions, peppers, tomatoes and ham. Unfortunately, it was also one of the most fat-laden selections. Here, I have cut the fat and cholesterol by reducing the number of eggs from four to two. One slice of crisp bacon adds just enough smoky flavor. All the good flavors the old farmers loved—egg, bacon and cheese—are still here, but without the guilt of overindulgence.

1   thick slice good-quality smoked bacon
1   teaspoon vegetable oil
¼   cup diced red or yellow onion
¼   cup diced red bell pepper
2   tablespoons diced green bell pepper
¼   cup diced, cored tomato
2   large eggs
    Pinch of salt
    Freshly ground black pepper
2   egg whites
    Vegetable-oil cooking spray
1   tablespoon coarsely shredded reduced-fat
      or whole-milk Cheddar cheese

1. Cook the bacon in a large (10-inch) nonstick skillet over medium heat until crisp; drain on a paper towel. Discard fat and wipe the skillet dry.

2. Add the oil, onion and red and green peppers to the skillet. Cook, stirring, over medium to medium-low heat until tender and lightly browned, about 5 minutes. Stir in the tomato, cover and cook 2 minutes. Transfer to a side dish, crumble the bacon and add to the cooked vegetables.

3. In a small bowl, whisk the eggs, a pinch of salt and a grinding of black pepper until frothy. In a separate bowl, whisk the whites until soft peaks form, add to the whole eggs and gently fold together just until blended.

4. Spray the skillet with vegetable-oil cooking spray; reheat over medium heat until hot enough to evaporate a drop of water immediately upon contact. Add the eggs and cook over medium-low heat until the eggs are set on the bottom, about 2 minutes. Cover and cook over low heat 1 minute. Spoon the reserved cooked vegetables evenly on the surface; sprinkle with the cheese. Carefully fold the omelet over the cheese. Cover and cook over low heat until set, about 2 minutes.

■ *If you are on a fat-restricted diet, reduced-fat Cheddar can provide one-third less fat than the regular Cheddar. Read the label carefully.*

159 CALORIES PER SERVING

12 G PROTEIN

10 G FAT

5 G CARBOHYDRATE

321 MG SODIUM

218 MG CHOLESTEROL

TIPS

SWEETENED
BREAKFAST OMELET

Makes 1 serving

✳ *Cut the fat considerably by
using a heavy nonstick pan.
Cooking in a nonstick pan can
eliminate at least two-thirds of
the grams of fat that come from
the butter or oil used to prevent
the food from sticking.*

✳ *Although many people
mistakenly associate all goat
cheese with the strong French
aged form, fresh goat cheese has
an entirely different taste. Mild,
with only a slight tang and a
deliciously creamy texture, goat
cheese has a low fat content,
containing only about 4 to 6
grams of fat per ounce, half
the amount in cream cheese.
A number of small, regional
producers have sprung up around
the country; check your grocer's
dairy case.*

THIS OMELET was inspired by a version once popular at restaurant brunches. The original was filled with high-fat cream cheese and sprinkled with confectioners' sugar. Because I like a touch of sweetness for breakfast, this omelet is a personal favorite. This lightened version uses mild fresh goat cheese, which is substantially lower in fat and cholesterol than cream cheese is. One large egg and two egg whites replace three whole eggs. For a more intense fresh-fruit flavor, use a fruit spread instead of the traditional sugar- or fruit-juice-sweetened jams or jellies.

2 egg whites
1 large egg
1 teaspoon unsalted butter or vegetable oil
2 tablespoons crumbled fresh goat cheese
1 tablespoon reduced-sugar fruit spread
   (apricot, strawberry or flavor of your choice)
½ teaspoon cinnamon sugar, or to taste

1. In a small bowl, whisk the egg whites and the egg until frothy; set aside. Heat the butter or oil over medium heat in a medium (8-to-10-inch) nonstick skillet; tip the skillet to coat evenly.

2. Add the eggs to the skillet and cook over medium heat until set around the edges, about 2 minutes. Lift the edges and allow the uncooked egg to run under the cooked portions. Sprinkle the goat cheese over the surface of the egg. Dot with the fruit spread, distributing evenly.

3. With a rubber spatula, carefully fold one-third of the omelet toward the center. Then fold the opposite side toward the center. Cook until the omelet is the desired consistency and then turn it out onto a serving plate.

4. Sprinkle the top with the cinnamon sugar and serve at once.

✳ *Cinnamon sugar is available in the spice section of supermarkets, or make your own by mixing ½ cup sugar with ½ teaspoon cinnamon.*

240 CALORIES PER SERVING

15 G PROTEIN

13 G FAT

15 G CARBOHYDRATE

276 MG SODIUM

237 MG CHOLESTEROL

ITALIAN-STYLE OMELET
with NEW POTATOES
(Frittata)
Makes 4 servings

✳ *Authentic Parmigiano-Reggiano, from the northern Italian region of Emilia Romagna, has not only the best taste because it has been aged longer but the lowest fat and cholesterol of all aged cheeses. It is made from partially skim milk.*

✳ *Vary this recipe by using whatever is on hand: chopped onions or mushrooms, bits of cooked sausage, chicken or other meats, leftover rice, pasta or cooked vegetables or fresh herbs.*

THE ITALIAN EQUIVALENT of the French omelet, called a frittata, is cooked flat rather than folded. It is served warm or at room temperature, cut into pie-shaped wedges. A frittata can be as plain—or as fancy—as the cook's mood or resources. Cut the cholesterol by substituting whites for some of the whole eggs.

1 tablespoon olive oil

1 cup cooked, cubed (½-inch) unpeeled new potatoes
   or any leftover cooked potatoes

½ cup diced (½-inch) red bell pepper

2 tablespoons finely chopped onion

1 teaspoon fresh thyme leaves, stripped from stems,
   or ¼ teaspoon dried
   Salt
   Freshly ground black pepper

4 large eggs

2 egg whites

1 tablespoon grated Parmesan cheese,
   preferably Parmigiano-Reggiano

2 tablespoons thinly sliced scallion tops

1. Heat the oil in a large (10-inch) nonstick skillet. Add the potatoes and cook, stirring, over medium-high heat until lightly browned on all sides, about 10 minutes. Reduce heat to medium; add the red pepper, onion and half the thyme; cook, stirring, until the peppers are lightly browned, about 5 minutes. Sprinkle with a pinch of salt and a grinding of black pepper; transfer to a side dish.

2. Whisk the eggs, egg whites, remaining thyme, another pinch of salt and another grinding of pepper. Reheat the pan until hot enough to sizzle the eggs. Pour the egg mixture into the hot pan and cook over medium heat until the edges begin to set, about 5 minutes. With a spatula, pull the set edges toward the center of the pan and tip the pan to let the uncooked egg run to the edges. Top with the cooked vegetables.

3. Meanwhile, preheat the broiler. Protect the handle of the skillet with a piece of foil if it isn't heatproof. Sprinkle the frittata with the grated Parmesan and scallion tops and place the skillet about 3 inches from the broiler. Broil until the top is golden, about 2 minutes.

4. To serve, loosen the sides of the frittata with a rubber spatula and slide out onto a round platter. Serve in wedges. It is good hot or at room temperature.

154 CALORIES PER SERVING

9 G PROTEIN

9 G FAT

9 G CARBOHYDRATE

188 MG SODIUM

214 MG CHOLESTEROL

OVEN-BAKED CINNAMON FRENCH TOAST

Makes 4 servings

* By adding liquid and sweetness, fruit juice helps retain the texture that might otherwise be compromised when the fat is reduced.

* Thick commercial Italian bread, toasted, is an acceptable substitute if you find yourself without good sourdough in the house.

* Apples higher in pectin— Golden Delicious, Granny Smith or Rome Beauties—make a chunkier sauce than do soft- textured apples like McIntosh, Cortland or Red Delicious.

FRENCH TOAST, soaked in whole eggs and sautéed in plenty of butter, is traditionally rich. Instead of being fried in butter, this version is baked in the oven in a minimum amount of melted butter. To create a more healthful breakfast, I also use low-fat milk and half the amount of whole eggs plus two egg whites. Apple juice helps compensate for the loss of flavor from fat. Bakery-quality whole-wheat Italian or mixed-wheat sourdough bread substitutes for the usual white. The topping of chunky applesauce more than makes up for the loss of saturated fat.

½ cup low-fat milk
¼ cup unsweetened apple juice
2 large eggs
2 egg whites
1 teaspoon ground cinnamon
1 teaspoon vanilla extract
8 half slices (each about ½ inch thick) from an 8-inch round loaf of whole-wheat Italian or mixed-wheat sourdough bread
1 teaspoon melted unsalted butter, or more if needed

Chunky Applesauce

1 tablespoon unsalted butter
3 cups cored, peeled and quartered apples, cut into ½-inch chunks
2 teaspoons sugar
½ cup unsweetened apple juice
Pinch of ground cinnamon

1. In a medium bowl, whisk the milk, apple juice, eggs, egg whites, cinnamon and vanilla until blended. Arrange the bread on a jelly roll pan or tray; pour the egg mixture evenly over the slices. Let stand, turning the bread with a spatula, until all the liquid is absorbed, about 20 minutes.

2. Preheat oven to 350 degrees F. Brush the melted butter over a large (15-x-10-inch) jelly roll pan or baking pan large enough to hold the French toast in one layer (or use two 13-x-9-inch baking pans). Add the soaked bread and bake until the bottom is browned, about 10 minutes. Carefully turn over and bake the other side until browned and puffed, about 15 minutes.

3. **Meanwhile, prepare the applesauce:** Heat 1 tablespoon butter in a large (10-to-12-inch) nonstick skillet over medium heat until foamy. Add the apples and sprinkle with the sugar. Cook, stirring, over medium-high heat until the apples begin to brown, about 10 minutes. Add the apple juice and cook, covered, stirring occasionally and partially mashing some of the apples, over medium-low heat until the apples are tender and make a chunky sauce, about 20 minutes. Sprinkle with the cinnamon.

4. Serve the French toast with Chunky Applesauce on the side.

257 CALORIES PER SERVING

9 G PROTEIN

8 G FAT

39 G CARBOHYDRATE

236 MG SODIUM

119 MG CHOLESTEROL

BANANA-OATMEAL PANCAKES

Makes 12 pancakes or 4 servings

TIP

✳ *Quick oats absorb moisture from the batter more slowly than do instant oats, allowing the pancakes to remain moist.*

314 CALORIES PER SERVING

7 G PROTEIN

12 G FAT

47 G CARBOHYDRATE

287 MG SODIUM

3 MG CHOLESTEROL

MENTION PANCAKES, and I think of the pancake house where I would, on occasion, dig into a stack slathered with butter and swimming in syrup. Prepared with white flour, butter and eggs, they were a far cry from this enlightened version. Here, I use a few tablespoons of oats—one of the most nutritious grains available—and an egg white instead of a whole egg. Bananas and low-fat milk provide moisture.

1	cup all-purpose flour
2	tablespoons rolled or quick-cooking (not instant) oats
2	teaspoons baking powder
¼	teaspoon ground cinnamon
	Pinch of salt
1	cup low-fat milk
3	tablespoons vegetable oil
2	tablespoons pure maple syrup
1	egg white
	Vegetable-oil cooking spray
1	cup sliced banana (about 1½ bananas)
	Raspberry & Maple Syrup (page 38) or
	Lemon-Cinnamon Honey (page 39)

1. In a large bowl, combine the flour, oats, baking powder, cinnamon and salt; stir to blend. In a separate bowl, combine the milk, oil, maple syrup and egg white; whisk until blended.

2. Pour the liquid ingredients over the dry and gently stir together just until blended. (The batter will be lumpy; do not overmix.)

3. Meanwhile, spray a very large (12-to-14-inch) nonstick skillet or griddle with vegetable-oil cooking spray. Heat over medium-high heat until hot enough to evaporate a drop of water immediately upon contact.

4. For each pancake, spoon ¼ cup of the batter onto the hot skillet or griddle. Cook just until a few bubbles begin to appear on the surface; arrange 3 or 4 slices of banana on each pancake. Continue to cook until the bottom is golden. Carefully turn over and cook the other side until golden, about 5 minutes per side. Keep warm while cooking the remaining pancakes.

5. Repeat with the remaining batter and banana slices. Serve topped with warm maple syrup or use Raspberry & Maple Syrup or Lemon-Cinnamon Honey.

COTTAGE CHEESE
& LEMON PANCAKES

Makes 14 small (3-inch) pancakes or 2 servings

STREAMLINE THE CALORIES usually found in pancake recipes by making a simple batter of an egg, an egg white, flour and a pinch of sugar and folding in low-fat cottage cheese and lemon zest.

TIP

✳ *Depending on the fat in the milk used to make them, cottage cheeses are far from equal: they are available in nonfat; 1 percent, with 1 gram of fat per ½ cup; 2 percent, with 2 grams of fat; and 4 percent, with 4 to 5 grams. For this recipe, use 1 percent cottage cheese.*

212 CALORIES PER SERVING

15 G PROTEIN

4 G FAT

27 G CARBOHYDRATE

430 MG SODIUM

110 MG CHOLESTEROL

1 large egg

1 egg white

¼ cup plus 2 tablespoons all-purpose flour

1 tablespoon sugar

2 tablespoons low-fat milk

1 teaspoon vanilla extract

½ cup low-fat cottage cheese

1 teaspoon grated or finely shredded lemon zest

Pinch of salt

Vegetable-oil cooking spray

Lemon-Cinnamon Honey (page 39) or
  Raspberry & Maple Syrup (page 38)

1. In a medium bowl, combine the whole egg, egg white, flour, sugar, milk and vanilla; stir just until blended. (The batter will be lumpy; do not overmix.) In a separate bowl, stir together the cottage cheese, lemon zest and salt until blended. Add to the batter and fold just until blended. (Don't be alarmed that the batter is lumpy.)

2. Spray a very large (12-to-14-inch) nonstick skillet or griddle with vegetable-oil cooking spray. Heat over medium-high heat until hot enough to evaporate a drop of water immediately upon contact.

3. For each pancake, spoon a heaping tablespoonful of batter onto the hot skillet or griddle. Cook until lightly browned and set on the bottom, about 2 minutes; using a thin spatula, carefully turn and brown the other side. Keep each batch warm and repeat with remaining batter.

4. Serve warm with Lemon-Cinnamon Honey or Raspberry & Maple Syrup.

HOT CEREAL *with* FRUIT & NUTS

Makes 4 servings

THIS OATMEAL CONTAINS A SURPRISING VARIANT—brown rice—which has a deliciously nutty quality. Lots of naturally sweet dried and fresh fruits add a measure of good taste without the fat traditionally derived from additions of butter and/or cream. When used sparingly, almonds are a healthier choice than butter as a topping; and brown sugar, Lemon-Cinnamon Honey or Raspberry & Maple Syrup add more flavor, not fat. Enough energy-producing carbohydrates are in a serving of this hot cereal to keep the body performing all morning.

1 cup water

1 cup skim milk

1 cup rolled oats

1 cup leftover cooked brown or white rice

1 cup diced, peeled and cored apples

2 tablespoons dark raisins

¼ teaspoon ground cinnamon

   Pinch of salt

½ cup fresh diced (¼-inch) peaches, fresh blueberries and/or raspberries

1 tablespoon sliced natural (unblanched) almonds, heated in a small skillet until toasted

   Brown sugar, Lemon-Cinnamon Honey (page 39) or Raspberry & Maple Syrup (page 38)

TIPS

* By weight, most nuts are 60 percent fat, so the almonds need to be used sparingly. Nuts contain no cholesterol.

* Because sugar is a carbohydrate and is more likely to be burned than stored as fat, it's better to top cereal with sweet syrups or brown sugar than with a large pat of butter.

* Brown rice has five times more vitamin E and three times more magnesium than white rice has.

* Natural (unblanched) almonds have the skins left on.

1. In a medium (3-quart) saucepan, combine the water, milk, oats, rice, apples, raisins, cinnamon and salt. Cook, stirring, over medium-low heat until the mixture boils and the cereal thickens, about 10 minutes.

2. Spoon into bowls and top each serving with peaches, blueberries and/or raspberries and the almonds.

3. Serve sprinkled with brown sugar or drizzled with Lemon-Cinnamon Honey or Raspberry & Maple Syrup.

216 CALORIES PER SERVING

7 G PROTEIN

3 G FAT

42 G CARBOHYDRATE

103 MG SODIUM

I MG CHOLESTEROL

THE BEST GRANOLA

Makes about 8 cups or 16 servings

* *Because nuts are high in fat, it's best to use fewer of them and more grains and dried fruit. Layering nonfat yogurt with granola as a sort of breakfast sundae is a good way to enjoy granola.*

* *Granola is also delicious with fresh bananas, kiwis and strawberries, topped with Vanilla Custard Sauce (page 257).*

* *The granola becomes soggy in humid weather; to keep it crunchy, store it in a tight tin.*

HOMEMADE GRANOLA is not only tastier than store-bought but gives the cook the opportunity to control the amount of fat added. Despite its image as a "healthy" cereal, granola, whether commercial or homemade, is by nature high in fat because of its nuts and seeds. Coconut, a common ingredient in most supermarket granolas, has a high ratio of saturated fat, so I have omitted it. I further reduced the sources of saturated fat by substituting vegetable oil for butter or shortening. Vary the nuts and dried fruit depending on what you have on hand. In fact, small amounts of dried fruit accumulating in the pantry are generally my cue that it's time to mix up a batch of granola.

4	cups rolled oats
½	cup sliced natural (unblanched) almonds
½	cup honey
½	cup molasses
¼	cup water
3	tablespoons vegetable oil
½	teaspoon ground cinnamon
½	cup raisins
½	cup diced dates or diced dried figs
½	cup diced prunes

1. Preheat oven to 325 degrees F. Combine the oats and almonds in a large bowl; stir to blend. In a small saucepan, combine the honey, molasses, water, vegetable oil and cinnamon; cook, stirring, until heated through, about 1 minute. Pour over the oat mixture and stir to blend.

2. Spread the granola in a large (15-x-10-inch) jelly roll pan. Bake until toasted, stirring every 10 minutes, 30 to 35 minutes.

3. Remove from the oven and stir in the raisins, dates or figs and prunes. Let cool completely. (The cereal becomes crisp as it cools.)

4. Serve with yogurt or skim milk and fresh fruit.

220 CALORIES PER ½-CUP SERVING

5 G PROTEIN

6 G FAT

40 G CARBOHYDRATE

5 MG SODIUM

0 MG CHOLESTEROL

BANANA WHOLE-WHEAT MUFFINS

Makes about 12 muffins

GRABBING A MUFFIN at the coffee shop on the way to work is often a sure way to blow any resolution to eat a more healthful diet. For although muffins are often touted as "healthy," they are frequently filled with butter. These contain a mere 2 tablespoons oil, with additional moisture added in the forms of mashed banana and low-fat yogurt. Vanilla contributes sweetness without extra sugar. Sprinkling the tops of the muffins with just a few pieces of chopped walnuts supplies the good taste without all the oil.

Vegetable-oil cooking spray
1 cup all-purpose flour
¾ cup whole-wheat flour
½ cup sugar
2 teaspoons baking powder
1 teaspoon baking soda
1 cup low-fat or nonfat plain yogurt
1 cup mashed ripe banana (approximately 2 medium)
2 tablespoons vegetable oil
1 extra-large egg
1 teaspoon vanilla extract
½ teaspoon grated lemon zest
¼ cup chopped walnuts, pecans or hazelnuts

1. Preheat oven to 400 degrees F. Spray muffin pans with vegetable-oil cooking spray.

2. In a large bowl, combine the flours, sugar, baking powder and baking soda; stir to blend.

TIPS

* *Whole-wheat flour absorbs more moisture than white flour. Therefore, when adding whole-wheat flour to muffins, remember that it should not be used in larger quantity than all-purpose flour or the muffins will be leaden.*

* *One large egg may be used in place of the extra-large.*

* *Bananas are an asset to the cook who wants to reduce fat in baked goods. In addition to being an excellent source of potassium, bananas have a creamy texture and buttery flavor and so can impart moisture and tenderness to baked goods, making them a suitable substitute for at least a portion of the fatty dairy products.*

3. In another bowl or large glass measuring cup, combine the yogurt, banana, oil, egg, vanilla and lemon zest; whisk to blend.

4. Pour the wet ingredients over the dry ingredients; stir just until blended. Do not overmix.

5. Spoon into the prepared pans, filling each cup about three-quarters full. Sprinkle the tops evenly with the chopped nuts.

6. Bake until the muffins are lightly browned and a toothpick inserted in the center comes out clean, 20 to 25 minutes. Cool slightly in pans. Turn out and cool on a wire rack.

169 CALORIES PER MUFFIN

5 G PROTEIN

5 G FAT

28 G CARBOHYDRATE

144 MG SODIUM

23 MG CHOLESTEROL

CINNAMON, DATE & BUTTERMILK WHOLE-WHEAT MUFFINS

Makes about 12 muffins

* *Muffin batter should always remain a little lumpy; if it is overmixed, the muffins will become tough, flat-topped or sunken.*

* *Fig & Prune Spread with Orange (page 42) is delicious with these muffins.*

* *One large egg may be used in place of the extra-large.*

Despite its name, buttermilk is nearly fat-free, made from cultured skim milk, not butter. Its name actually derives from what it is not: it used to be made from milk skimmed from the butter-making process. (Now it is cultured from skim milk.) Its tanginess adds flavor, and in combination with leavening, it produces a tender, light crumb in baked goods. Whole-wheat flour and wheat germ are both far better sources of protein, vitamins and minerals than all-purpose flour. Dried dates are a good source of fiber.

	Vegetable-oil cooking spray
1	cup whole-wheat flour
1	cup all-purpose flour
¼	cup wheat germ
2	teaspoons baking powder
1	teaspoon baking soda
1½	teaspoons ground cinnamon
½	cup chopped dates
1¼	cups buttermilk
½	cup packed light brown sugar
¼	cup vegetable oil
1	extra-large egg
1	teaspoon vanilla extract

1. Preheat oven to 400 degrees F. Spray muffin pans with vegetable-oil cooking spray.

2. In a large bowl, combine the flours, wheat germ, baking powder, baking soda, cinnamon and dates; stir to blend.

3. In another bowl, combine the buttermilk, brown sugar, vegetable oil, egg and vanilla; whisk until thoroughly blended.

4. Pour the wet ingredients over the dry ingredients; stir just until blended. Do not overmix.

5. Spoon into the prepared muffin pans, filling each cup about three-quarters full. Bake until the muffins are lightly browned and a toothpick inserted in the center comes out clean, about 20 minutes. Cool slightly in pans. Turn out and cool on a wire rack.

196 CALORIES PER MUFFIN

5 G PROTEIN

6 G FAT

32 G CARBOHYDRATE

161 MG SODIUM

23 MG CHOLESTEROL

MOLASSES & RAISIN BRAN MUFFINS

Makes about 12 muffins

TIP

✳ *One large egg may be used in place of the extra-large.*

181 CALORIES PER MUFFIN

4 G PROTEIN

5 G FAT

32 G CARBOHYDRATE

238 MG SODIUM

23 MG CHOLESTEROL

HERE IS A BRAN MUFFIN that is moist and tender, without being high in fat. Low-fat yogurt and molasses add moisture and flavor. These muffins are fiber- and nutrient-dense with whole-grain cereal and raisins.

Vegetable-oil cooking spray
1 cup shredded bran cereal (All-Bran)
1 cup low-fat or nonfat plain yogurt
½ cup whole-wheat flour
½ cup all-purpose flour
2 teaspoons baking powder
1 teaspoon baking soda
1 teaspoon ground cinnamon
1 cup seedless raisins
¼ cup vegetable oil
½ cup dark molasses
1 extra-large egg
1 teaspoon vanilla extract

1. Preheat oven to 400 degrees F. Spray muffin pans with vegetable-oil cooking spray.

2. In a small bowl, stir the bran cereal and yogurt together. Set aside while assembling the remaining ingredients.

3. In a large bowl, combine the flours, baking powder, baking soda and cinnamon; stir to blend. Add the raisins and stir until separated and coated with the flour mixture.

4. In a large (2-cup) liquid measuring cup or a small bowl, combine the oil, molasses, egg and vanilla; whisk to blend.

5. Add the bran and yogurt mixture and the liquid ingredients to the flour mixture. Fold until the batter is evenly moistened. Spoon into the prepared pans, filling each cup about three-quarters full.

6. Bake until a toothpick inserted in the center comes out clean, about 20 minutes. Cool slightly in pans. Turn out and cool on a wire rack.

RASPBERRY & MAPLE SYRUP

Makes about 1 cup

57 CALORIES PER TABLESPOON

0 G PROTEIN

0 G FAT

15 G CARBOHYDRATE

20 MG SODIUM

0 MG CHOLESTEROL

FOR THE BEST FLAVOR, be sure to use pure maple syrup. Store in a small jar in the refrigerator for up to one month.

1   cup pure maple syrup
½   cup fresh or unsweetened frozen raspberries

1. Combine the maple syrup and raspberries in a small saucepan. Heat, stirring, over medium heat until boiling. Reduce heat and simmer over low heat 5 minutes.

2. Strain the syrup through a sieve set over a bowl; press down on the raspberries to extract as much of the flavor and juice as possible. Discard the seeds.

3. Serve warm or at room temperature.

LEMON-CINNAMON HONEY

Makes about 1 cup

THIS IS WONDERFUL drizzled over pancakes or French toast, added to a cup of tea or sipped from a spoon when you feel a cold coming on.

1 cup mild-flavored honey
¼ cup fresh lemon juice
¼ teaspoon ground cinnamon

1. In a small saucepan, combine the honey, lemon juice and cinnamon. Heat, stirring, over low heat, just until the ingredients are warm and blended.

2. Serve warm over pancakes or French toast or keep cold and drizzle on toast.

TIPS

✳ *For a refreshing drink, stir a little into a glass of ice water.*

✳ *It may be stored in the refrigerator for up to one month.*

66 CALORIES PER TABLESPOON

0 G PROTEIN

0 G FAT

17 G CARBOHYDRATE

1 MG SODIUM

0 MG CHOLESTEROL

CRANBERRY–RAISIN SPREAD

Makes about 2½ cups

HOMEMADE FRUIT SPREADS are healthful alternatives to the traditional fat-laden spreads of cream cheese and butter. Cranberries, native to North America, are an excellent source of vitamin C. Here, they are partially sweetened with raisins and apple juice.

1	12-ounce bag cranberries
1	cup golden raisins
1½	cups cranberry-juice cocktail or apple juice
½-¾	cup sugar
¼	teaspoon ground cloves

1. Place all ingredients in a medium saucepan. Bring to a boil over high heat.

2. Reduce heat and simmer, stirring occasionally and pressing down on the berries to break them, for 15 minutes or until thick.

3. Pour into a bowl, cool, cover and refrigerate.

APRICOT-GINGER
SPREAD

Makes about 3 cups

THIS TANGY SPREAD, with the fresh, smart taste of ginger, is wonderful on muffins, toast or even as a filling for an omelet.

12	ounces dried apricots
1	tablespoon plus 1 teaspoon peeled, minced fresh gingerroot, or more to taste
2½	cups apple juice
1	cup water

23 CALORIES PER TABLESPOON

0 G PROTEIN

0 G FAT

6 G CARBOHYDRATE

1 MG SODIUM

0 MG CHOLESTEROL

1. Oil the blade of a food processor. Place the apricots in the container and pulse the processor until they are in small pieces (less than ¼-inch).

2. Place all ingredients in a medium saucepan. Bring to a boil over high heat.

3. Reduce heat and simmer, stirring occasionally, for 15 minutes until the mixture is thick and the apricots are soft.

4. Pour into a bowl, cool, cover and refrigerate.

FIG & PRUNE SPREAD
with ORANGE

Makes about 2 cups

THIS DRIED-FRUIT SPREAD is virtually fat-free and so flavorful that when you spread it on warm toast, you won't miss the butter.

1   cup diced (¼-inch) dried figs
1   cup diced (¼-inch) prunes
2   cups orange juice
2   teaspoons grated orange zest

1. Place all ingredients in a medium saucepan. Bring to a boil over high heat.

2. Reduce heat and simmer, stirring frequently, for 15 minutes.

3. Increase the heat and stir constantly until all of the liquid has been absorbed.

4. Spoon into a bowl, cool, cover and refrigerate.

ICED PEACH *or* MANGO
MILK SHAKE

Makes 1 serving

THIS REFRESHING LOW-CALORIE, naturally sweet drink makes a great snack and a nutritious, quick breakfast.

1½   cups peeled, pitted and coarsely chopped ripe peach or mango (1 large)

1 cup low-fat milk
¼ cup orange juice
2-3 ice cubes

240 CALORIES PER SERVING

10 G PROTEIN

3 G FAT

47 G CARBOHYDRATE

124 MG SODIUM

10 MG CHOLESTEROL

1. In a blender jar, combine the peach or mango, milk, orange juice and ice cubes; puree until smooth.

2. Pour into a tall glass and serve with a straw.

STRAWBERRY-YOGURT SMOOTHIE

Makes 1 serving

ANOTHER NICE WAY to start the day, particularly in the summer, when fresh strawberries are available. This blender drink is especially rich in calcium.

1 cup plain low-fat yogurt
1 cup sliced, hulled strawberries
½ cup cranberry-juice cocktail
2-3 ice cubes
2-3 teaspoons sugar (optional)

261 CALORIES PER SERVING

13 G PROTEIN

4 G FAT

45 G CARBOHYDRATE

165 MG SODIUM

14 MG CHOLESTEROL

1. In a blender jar, combine the yogurt, strawberries, cranberry juice and ice cubes; puree until smooth. Taste and add sugar if desired.

2. Pour into a tall glass and serve with a straw.

Chapter 2

APPETIZERS &
SNACKS

APPETIZERS & SNACKS

I CAN'T COUNT HOW MANY TIMES I have vowed not to succumb to snacking between meals, only to arrive home famished and tear into a bag of chips. Or the times I have walked into a party resolved to eat in moderation and come face-to-face with a giant wedge of my favorite triple crème blue-veined cheese, perfectly ripened and beckoning from the buffet table.

Like other Americans—who spend $1.8 billion dollars just on potato chips in a single year—I love to snack. Unfortunately, though, few of the appetizers I crave live up to their name. Instead of getting my palate excited for what lies ahead, they take over and become a meal in themselves—and an unhealthy one at that.

Although the bag brags that they are "cholesterol-free," potato chips contain about 150 calories per ounce, with about 60 percent of them from fat. For its part, blue cheese is as close to pure butter as I can get—though, of course, I try not to think about that when I'm smearing it on my cracker.

Properly conceived, however, chips and dips don't have to be disastrous intermissions in otherwise smart diets. With a little culinary creativity in fat-saving techniques—and a lively mix of fresh vegetables, herbs and spices—it is easy to prepare satisfying snacks and appetizers that take the edge off hunger without ruining one's resolve to eat right.

VEGETABLES, FOR INSTANCE, become enticements to the rest of the dinner when their naturally low-fat attributes are not sunk by overly rich preparations and toppings. Crisp oven-roasted potato skins topped with a sparkling salsa instead of being fried and served dripping with cheese present a triumph of health over fat. Even the beloved avocado can be cajoled into delivering less fat when it is mashed and stretched with crunchy vegetables, while the eggplant, whose spongelike properties would make it invaluable at an offshore oil spill, takes nicely to a light brushing of olive oil and a hot oven.

In place of rich, creamy French cheeses or the ubiquitous cream cheese, fresh goat cheese is low in fat, yet pleasantly moist and tangy enough to be interesting. For a sweeter effect, I like skim-milk ricotta or low-fat cottage cheese that has been whipped for a while in the food processor to make it creamy.

These innovations have produced a variety of dips at my coffee table: spicy black bean; low-fat blue cheese; a shrimp-filled, dill-seasoned spread; hummus made of chick-peas with garlic and lemon juice; and an onion dip from real caramelized onions, not packaged powder. All are light-years lower in fat than the usual cream-cheese-and-sour-cream blends. Even potato chips have been superceded by some crunchy pita chips that most people find equally irresistible.

Dips & Chips

New Hummus . . . 49

Poor Man's Caviar (Roasted Eggplant Dip) . . . 50

Guacamole . . . 52

Black Bean Dip . . . 53

Onion Dip . . . 54

Seasoned Tortilla Chips . . . 55

Pita Chips . . . 56

Finger Foods

Red Pepper Wedges Stuffed with Tuna . . . 57

Stuffed Mushrooms . . . 58

Deviled Eggs with Curried Potato . . . 60

Potted Shrimp Canapés . . . 62

Buffalo Chicken Strips with Blue Cheese Dip & Celery Sticks . . . 64

Potato Skins with Salsa & Cheese . . . 66

Crisp Garlic Potato Skins . . . 68

Celery Stuffed with Blue Cheese . . . 69

NEW HUMMUS

Makes about 1½ cups

HUMMUS, THE GARLICKY, UNCTUOUSLY SMOOTH DIP that is a staple in the Middle East and at North American parties, is made from a combination of chick-peas, a nutritious legume, and tahini, a fatty paste of toasted ground sesame seeds. To satisfy health-conscious tastes, I deployed the primary flavorings in hummus—lemon juice, garlic, olive oil, mint and dill—but left the fatty tahini behind.

TIP

✳ *Hummus is also excellent as a sandwich stuffing. Fill a pita half with hummus, tomatoes, sprouts and lettuce.*

33 CALORIES PER TABLESPOON

I G PROTEIN

2 G FAT

4 G CARBOHYDRATE

90 MG SODIUM

0 MG CHOLESTEROL

1   can (19 ounces) chick-peas or garbanzo beans,
        thoroughly rinsed and drained
2   tablespoons fresh lemon juice
2   tablespoons extra-virgin olive oil
2   tablespoons cold water
2   garlic cloves, finely chopped
     Salt to taste
     Cayenne pepper
1   tablespoon *each* chopped fresh mint,
        parsley and dill

1. Puree the chick-peas or garbanzo beans, lemon juice, olive oil, water and garlic in a food processor until smooth and fluffy. Add salt to taste.

2. Transfer to a shallow soup bowl or other deep-sided plate. Smooth the top with a spatula. Sprinkle lightly with the cayenne and top with the chopped herbs.

3. Serve with Pita Chips (page 56) or with vegetable crudités.

POOR MAN'S CAVIAR

(Roasted Eggplant Dip)

Makes about 1¼ cups

WHETHER MADE AT HOME or purchased in tubs from the dairy section of the supermarket, most dips are cream-based. Some of the most flavorful dips, however, are made primarily of vegetables. This recipe uses eggplant, one of my favorites. Because it is usually fried in olive oil, eggplant has earned a reputation for absorbing too much fat during cooking. Here, it is drizzled with a minimum of olive oil and oven-roasted. It is then finely chopped and combined with other oven-roasted vegetables so that it becomes a robust-tasting dip or spread. Serve with vegetables, toasted bread or crackers.

½   medium (about 1¼ pounds) eggplant

1   large red bell pepper, quartered and seeded

1   head of garlic, unpeeled, separated into cloves

1   tablespoon extra-virgin olive oil

2   teaspoons fresh lemon juice

1   tablespoon chopped fresh basil or fresh parsley

½   teaspoon fresh thyme leaves, stripped from stems,
    or ¼ teaspoon dried

¼   teaspoon salt, or to taste
    Freshly ground black pepper to taste

1. Preheat oven to 350 degrees F. Place the eggplant, red pepper and unpeeled garlic cloves in a 13-x-9-inch baking dish; drizzle with the oil; stir to coat. Roast until the eggplant is browned and the peppers are soft, about 45 minutes, turning the vegetables frequently.

2. Let stand until cool enough to handle. Peel the eggplant, pepper and garlic and finely chop. Transfer to a medium bowl; add any oil left in the baking dish.

3. Add the lemon juice, basil or parsley, thyme, salt and a grinding of black pepper; stir vigorously until blended.

4. Serve in a small dish and spread on crackers or toasted Italian bread; or use as a dip with Pita Chips (page 56).

GUACAMOLE

Makes about 3 cups

TIP

❋ *Kirby cucumbers are small, about 4 inches long, and are usually used for pickling. They have fewer seeds than regular cucumbers and are firmer, crunchier and less watery. If you can't find them, you can substitute seedless or seeded regular cucumbers.*

8 CALORIES PER TABLESPOON

0 G PROTEIN

0.6 G FAT

1 G CARBOHYDRATE

23 MG SODIUM

0 MG CHOLESTEROL

MANY TRADITIONAL GUACAMOLE RECIPES, especially those made with sour cream, are loaded with fat. Avocado, the basis for every guacamole, is a concentrated source of vegetable fat. To reduce fat, I have omitted the sour cream and used just one mashed avocado. Diced tomatoes, cucumbers and red onion added to the basic combination of avocado, jalapeño, lime juice and cilantro contribute lots of freshness and crunch and increase the quantity of the recipe. The result: guilt-free guacamole.

1 ripe avocado, peeled, halved and pitted

1 cup diced (¼-inch) plum tomato

½ cup diced (¼-inch) Kirby cucumber or seedless cucumber

½ cup diced (¼-inch) red onion

2 tablespoons fresh lime juice

2 tablespoons chopped fresh cilantro

1 tablespoon seeded, minced jalapeño or other chili pepper, or to taste

½ teaspoon salt, or to taste

1. Dice the avocado flesh into small (approximately ¼-inch) pieces. Add the tomato, cucumber, red onion, lime juice, cilantro, jalapeño and salt.

2. Stir with a spoon until the mixture is blended and the avocado is roughly mashed.

3. Serve as a dip with Seasoned Tortilla Chips (page 55) or Pita Chips (page 56).

BLACK BEAN DIP

Makes about 1¼ cups

TIP

B LACK BEAN DIPS often contain quantities of fat, added to make them smooth and more flavorful. This pungent dip, however, is essentially fat-free. To infuse the beans with flavor, they are simply pureed with chicken broth, lime juice, chili powder and cumin. As an extra advantage, this recipe uses convenient canned beans. Serve with vegetables or toasted tortilla chips.

* *You can substitute canned beans, rinsed to remove their salt and tinny flavor, for dried in all quick-cooked bean dishes, saving hours of time. Jalapeño pepper, fresh cilantro and spices will perk them up nicely.*

1	teaspoon chili powder
½	teaspoon ground cumin
1	can (19 ounces) black beans, thoroughly rinsed and drained
1	tablespoon fresh lime juice
¼	cup reduced-sodium or homemade chicken broth (page 75) or water
¼	cup finely diced red bell pepper, seeds, stem and ribs removed
2	tablespoons seeded, finely diced jalapeño pepper
1	tablespoon chopped fresh cilantro

37 CALORIES PER TABLESPOON

2 G PROTEIN

0.2 G FAT

7 G CARBOHYDRATE

15 MG SODIUM

0 MG CHOLESTEROL

1. Heat the chili powder and cumin in a small skillet, stirring constantly, over low heat, just until fragrant, about 1 minute.

2. Place the spices, beans, lime juice and broth in the bowl of a food processor and process until the texture is chunky-smooth.

3. Transfer to a medium bowl and add the red pepper, jalapeño and cilantro. Taste and correct seasoning, if desired. Serve with Seasoned Tortilla Chips (page 55) or vegetable crudités.

ONION DIP

Makes about 1 cup

CHANCES ARE MOST OF US have eaten our share of that American proverbial favorite, instant onion-soup mix and sour cream. As good as the dip once tasted, the thought of it now sends my guilt barometer soaring. To achieve the caramelized onion flavor that I love, I slowly cooked onions in a little oil, then stirred them into a smooth, creamy low-fat mixture of pureed ricotta and cottage cheese. The delicious results did not become apparent until I let the dip sit refrigerated overnight; the flavors develop considerably upon standing. My lucky "accident" lacks not only much of the fat of its predecessor but also the chemical-tasting overtones of the packaged mix.

1	teaspoon vegetable oil
1½	cups finely chopped onions
3	tablespoons water
½	cup low-fat ricotta
½	cup low-fat cottage cheese
¼	teaspoon salt, or to taste
¼	teaspoon freshly ground black pepper, or to taste

1. Heat oil in a medium (8-to-10-inch) nonstick skillet over medium heat. Add the onions and water, lower heat and cook, stirring occasionally, until the onions turn dark golden-brown, about 30 minutes.

2. Meanwhile, place the ricotta and cottage cheese in the bowl of a food processor and process until smooth.

3. Toss the onions with the salt and pepper and stir gently into the cheese mixture. Refrigerate the dip up to 1 day or for at least 2 hours before serving.

TIPS

❋ *For best results, make this at least 24 hours ahead.*

❋ *Adding a little liquid— water, wine or chicken stock— when sautéing vegetables is the best way to prevent them from sticking without adding fat.*

❋ *Ricotta is available in whole-milk, part-skim, low-fat or fat-free forms. Whole-milk ricotta has 4 grams of fat per ounce, part-skim has 3, and low-fat has 2 grams.*

24 CALORIES PER TABLESPOON

2 G PROTEIN

I G FAT

2 G CARBOHYDRATE

72 MG SODIUM

3 MG CHOLESTEROL

SEASONED TORTILLA CHIPS

Makes 24 chips

FRESH FLOUR AND CORN TORTILLAS are available in the dairy sections of many supermarkets. The thinnest tortillas make the best chips. These are a great-tasting, easy-to-make, low-fat alternative to commercial tortilla chips.

29 CALORIES PER CHIP

1 G PROTEIN

1 G FAT

4 G CARBOHYDRATE

1 MG SODIUM

0 MG CHOLESTEROL

6   thin flour or corn tortillas
     (approximately 6 inches in diameter)
1   tablespoon vegetable oil
1½ teaspoons cumin seeds, crushed with a mortar
     and pestle or chopped with a knife,
     or 3 tablespoons finely chopped onion

1. Preheat oven to 350 degrees F.

2. Brush both sides of each tortilla with the oil. Sprinkle with either the cumin seeds or the chopped onion. Stack and cut into six triangular wedges.

3. Arrange in a single layer on a nonstick baking sheet. Bake until golden and crisp, 12 to 15 minutes.

4. Serve warm with Guacamole (page 52), Black Bean Dip (page 53) or any dip of your choice.

PITA CHIPS

Makes 16 chips

TIPS

✳ *Stow any dry pitas in the freezer until you have enough on hand to make the chips. They are so good, you may end up buying pitas especially to make chips.*

✳ *This recipe can easily be doubled or tripled. Store the chips in plastic bags at room temperature.*

18 CALORIES PER CHIP

I G PROTEIN

0.6 G FAT

3 G CARBOHYDRATE

27 MG SODIUM

0 MG CHOLESTEROL

WE ALL LOVE CHIPS. But don't be misled by bags marked "no cholesterol." Unless the chips have been fried in animal fat, they never contain cholesterol, but they are nonetheless highly oily, because they are fried. And regardless of its source, fat is fat. These oven-toasted pita chips prove just as irresistible as potato chips, yet contain little oil. They are so easy to make that you will wonder why anyone would buy commercially prepared chips.

> 2 pita breads
> 2 teaspoons olive oil
> ½ garlic clove, crushed through a press

1. Preheat oven to 350 degrees F.

2. Using a small knife or kitchen scissors, cut along the folded circumference of the pita breads to create four circles of bread.

3. Combine the olive oil and garlic in a small bowl; lightly brush it on the outside of the surface of the bread. Stack the circles of bread and cut the stack into pie-shaped wedges.

4. Arrange in a single layer on a nonstick baking sheet. Bake until golden, about 8 to 10 minutes. Serve with Poor Man's Caviar (page 50) or any dip of your choice.

RED PEPPER WEDGES STUFFED *with* TUNA

Makes 8 servings

DIPS AND SPREADS MADE OF FISH are tastier than cream-based ones, so it's surprising that so few people think of making them. This dip takes its inspiration from a popular dip in the south of France called tapenade. But while the original is made primarily of black olives, which are oily, I made mine mainly with water-packed tuna, seasoned with Mediterranean accents.

1   can (6½ ounces) water-packed white tuna, very well drained
1   garlic clove, finely chopped
1   tablespoon finely chopped yellow onion
2   tablespoons extra-virgin olive oil
2   tablespoons pitted, minced Kalamata or
       other brine-cured black olives
1   tablespoon small capers, drained
1   tablespoon minced red onion
1   tablespoon finely diced tomato flesh
¼   teaspoon chopped fresh rosemary, or pinch dried
2   large red bell peppers, seeded and cut into sixteen 1-inch wedges
       Sprigs fresh rosemary or chopped Italian (flat-leaf) parsley

1. Place the tuna, garlic, yellow onion and oil in the bowl of a food processor. Process until smooth.

2. Transfer the tuna mixture to a medium bowl and add the olives, capers, red onion, tomato and rosemary; stir until blended.

3. Spoon a tablespoon of the mixture into each pepper wedge and garnish each piece with a sprig of fresh rosemary or some chopped parsley.

TIPS

✳ *You may want to make extras. My experience is that you can't keep these on the plate at a party.*

✳ *Water-packed tuna offers a huge savings of fat compared with oil-packed tuna, for it contains only 1 gram of fat per 3-ounce serving, while the oil-packed variety contains 8 to 12 fat grams in the same amount.*

69 CALORIES PER SERVING
6 G PROTEIN
4 G FAT
2 G CARBOHYDRATE
106 MG SODIUM
10 MG CHOLESTEROL

STUFFED MUSHROOMS

Makes 4 servings

TIPS

✳ *For information about fresh goat cheese, see page 18.*

✳ *Sun-dried tomatoes pack an enormous amount of flavor. Although they may seem expensive when priced by the pound, one or two will richly flavor a dish, adding depth and sweetness. Their meaty intensity is especially useful in winter, when ripe, tasty tomatoes are all but impossible to find. Avoid the ones packed in oil, however: they are high in fat.*

ON THEIR OWN, mushrooms are not particularly flavorful. Perhaps this is why they are often stuffed with ingredients that include heavy cream, cream cheese or bread crumbs laden with butter. These mushrooms, however, are filled with fresh goat cheese, a low-fat alternative, which has been seasoned with herbs, shallots cooked in a minimum of olive oil and sun-dried tomatoes.

9   large white button mushrooms (about 10 ounces)
2   teaspoons olive oil
2   tablespoons finely chopped shallots
1   cup washed, trimmed, chopped and packed fresh spinach
     leaves
1   tablespoon finely chopped sun-dried tomatoes
1   teaspoon fresh thyme leaves, stripped from stems,
     or ½ teaspoon dried
2   tablespoons crumbled fresh goat cheese
     Pinch of salt
     Freshly ground black pepper

1. Break the stems off 8 of the mushrooms. Finely chop the stems and the remaining whole mushroom; set aside.

2. Preheat oven to 350 degrees F. Lightly brush a 9-inch pie plate or other baking dish and the outside of the mushroom caps with 1 teaspoon of the olive oil. Arrange the caps in the prepared baking dish smooth side down.

3. Combine the remaining 1 teaspoon olive oil, the finely chopped mushroom stems and the shallots in a medium (8-to-10-inch) nonstick skillet. Cook, stirring, over medium-low heat until the mushrooms and shallots are very tender, about 4 minutes. Add the spinach, sun-dried tomatoes and thyme; cook, stirring, until the spinach is wilted, about 3 minutes. Remove from heat and stir in the goat cheese, salt and black pepper.

4. Spoon about 1 tablespoon of the spinach mixture into each mushroom cap. Cover with foil and bake 15 minutes. Uncover and bake until the mushrooms are tender, about 10 minutes.

73 CALORIES PER SERVING

3 G PROTEIN

4 G FAT

9 G CARBOHYDRATE

107 MG SODIUM

4 MG CHOLESTEROL

DEVILED EGGS
with CURRIED POTATO

Makes 1 cup filling,
enough for 16 egg-white halves or 8 servings

58 CALORIES PER SERVING

6 G PROTEIN

2 G FAT

5 G CARBOHYDRATE

76 MG SODIUM

34 MG CHOLESTEROL

DEVILED EGGS, hard-boiled eggs that are halved and stuffed with the yolks that have been mashed with mayonnaise and seasonings, are synonymous with buffet tables. Because of the high levels of cholesterol in the yolks, eggs have fallen from grace. Yet they remain a nutritious, wholesome food and are harmless when eaten in moderation. In this recipe, the hard-cooked whites, which contain no fat, are filled with a mixture that contains only one yolk, stretched with a smooth mixture of potatoes mashed with ginger, curry and garlic. Delicious!

8	extra-large or large eggs
1	teaspoon olive or vegetable oil
2	teaspoons finely chopped garlic
½	teaspoon peeled, grated fresh gingerroot
2	tablespoons water or broth
1	teaspoon curry powder
1	cup diced cooked potatoes
¼	cup low-fat plain yogurt
1	tablespoon thinly sliced chives or scallion tops
	Salt to taste

1. Cover the unshelled eggs with cold water and bring to a boil over medium-low heat. Reduce heat and simmer, covered, for 15 minutes. Remove from heat and chill the eggs in cold water.

2. Remove the shells from the eggs; halve lengthwise. Scoop out the yolks, reserving one for filling (discard the rest). Place the whites, hollowed sides up, on a large plate.

3. Heat the oil in a small (6-to-8-inch) skillet over medium-low heat. Add the garlic and ginger and sauté gently until soft, about 3 minutes. Add the water or broth and curry powder; continue cooking, stirring, until the mixture becomes a thick paste, another 2 minutes. Remove from heat.

4. In a medium bowl, combine the potatoes, curry paste, yogurt, reserved hard-boiled egg yolk and chives or scallions; mash with a potato masher until smooth and completely combined.

5. Spoon or pipe 1 tablespoon of the mixture into each hard-boiled egg-white half.

TIP

✳ *Confusingly, farmer cheese can refer to two very different types of low-fat cheese, which are not interchangeable. One type, the one required for this recipe, is a semi-solid, crumbly cheese that is much like a cottage cheese with the whey pressed out and resembles feta cheese. The other kind, not to be used here, is a Colby-type firm cheese.*

15 CALORIES PER TABLESPOON

3 G PROTEIN

0.3 G FAT

0 G CARBOHYDRATE

41 MG SODIUM

22 MG CHOLESTEROL

POTTED SHRIMP CANAPÉS

Makes 1½ cups or enough for 24 servings

THE TRADITIONAL VERSION OF THIS SPREAD consists of butter creamed together with chopped shrimp and spread on small sandwiches and crackers. The canapé is just as elegant and delicious—and much better for you—when the cooked shrimp are combined with farmer cheese, a soft-curd, low-fat cheese. If it is not available in your region, substitute low-fat cottage cheese or ricotta that has been drained in a sieve for at least 24 hours.

1 bay leaf

1 thick onion slice

½ teaspoon salt

¾ pound medium shrimp, peeled and deveined

3¼ ounces (½ cup) farmer cheese (half of a 6½-ounce package)

2 tablespoons chopped fresh dill or 1 tablespoon fresh parsley chopped with ½ teaspoon dried dill

1 tablespoon fresh lemon juice

½ teaspoon grated lemon zest

Pinch of allspice

Salt

Freshly ground black pepper

Snipped fresh dill

Toasts, celery boats, slices of seedless cucumber and/or hollowed cherry tomatoes

1. Half fill a medium (3-quart) saucepan with water; add the bay leaf, onion and salt; cover and heat to boiling. Stir in the shrimp; cook, uncovered, over high heat until the water returns to a boil and the shrimp are opaque in the center, about 5 minutes. Drain immediately and rinse with cold water. Remove bay leaf and onion. Dry the shrimp on a paper towel.

2. Coarsely chop the shrimp in the bowl of a food processor. There should be about 1 cup, packed. Transfer to a medium bowl.

3. Combine the cheese, dill or parsley, lemon juice, lemon zest and allspice in the food processor; process until very smooth. Add to the shrimp; stir until well blended.

4. Add salt and pepper to taste. Spoon into a small crock or serving bowl and smooth the top. Sprinkle the top with chopped dill. Spread the potted shrimp on toasts, celery boats or thick slices of cucumber or stuff into cherry tomatoes. Garnish each canapé with snipped fresh dill.

TIP

❋ *The simple step of removing the skin from chicken breasts cuts the fat by half.*

171 CALORIES PER SERVING

13 G PROTEIN

1 G FAT

4 G CARBOHYDRATE

505 MG SODIUM

50 MG CHOLESTEROL

BUFFALO CHICKEN STRIPS
with BLUE CHEESE DIP
& CELERY STICKS

Makes 4 servings (about ¾ cup blue cheese dip)

TRADITIONALLY, BUFFALO CHICKEN WINGS are made from deep-fried wings cooked with the skin left on. Replacing the deep-fried wings with quickly seared strips of breast meat eliminates most of the fat. The flavor, however, is just as fiery as ever. Depending on your taste, use Louisiana hot sauce, which is just a little more mellow than Tabasco, or if you can take the heat, use the hotter Tabasco. The fat and calories in the dip are tempered here by substituting yogurt and buttermilk for the usual sour cream.

8   ounces chicken breasts, trimmed,
 cut lengthwise into ½-inch strips
 Vegetable-oil cooking spray
 Pinch of salt
 Freshly ground black pepper
2   tablespoons butter
2   tablespoons hot sauce, or to taste
 Celery sticks

Blue Cheese Dip
⅓   cup low-fat plain yogurt
¼   cup buttermilk
2   ounces blue cheese, finely crumbled
 Pinch of salt
 Freshly ground black pepper

1. Remove the white tendon running through each chicken breast. Spray a large (10-to-12-inch) nonstick skillet with vegetable-oil cooking spray; heat until hot enough to sizzle a strip of chicken. Add all the chicken and quickly sear both sides until the chicken is cooked through, about 3 minutes. Remove to a side dish; sprinkle with salt and pepper.

2. Off the heat, add the butter to the hot skillet and stir until melted. Stir in the hot sauce until blended. Add the cooked chicken and stir-fry over medium-high heat just until the chicken is coated with the sauce. Transfer to a platter and arrange with the celery sticks.

3. **Making the blue cheese dip:** Stir the yogurt, buttermilk, blue cheese, salt and a grinding of black pepper together. Spoon into a small bowl and serve with the chicken and celery sticks.

POTATO SKINS *with* SALSA & CHEESE

Makes 4 servings

TIPS

✳ *Although potatoes have earned a bad reputation among dieters, it has always been what was put on the potato—fatty additions like butter, sour cream, bacon and cheese—that was the problem, not the potato itself. Potatoes are high in carbo-hydrates, not fat, and even contain lots of vitamin C. Much of that nutritive value resides in the skin.*

✳ *You can substitute frozen or canned corn for the fresh.*

180 CALORIES PER SERVING

4 G PROTEIN

9 G FAT

23 G CARBOHYDRATE

105 MG SODIUM

2 MG CHOLESTEROL

WHEN I WAS A YOUNG SKIER, I would bite into a plate of deep-fried potato skins dripping with melted cheese, bacon and sour cream and rationalize that I could burn off the calories on my next run down the slopes. Their fat content—an issue rarely considered then—is inescapable, however. This revision captures the crunch by brushing the skins lightly with olive oil and crisping them under the broiler. The topping is a fresh salsa sprinkled with cheese. After the taste, the best part is being able to indulge—without having to ski at breakneck speed later.

2 large russet potatoes

¾ cup diced, seeded, firm, ripe tomato

½ cup fresh corn kernels (cut from cob)

¼ cup rinsed, drained canned black beans

2 tablespoons finely chopped seedless or Kirby cucumber

2 tablespoons thinly sliced scallion

2 tablespoons olive oil

1 tablespoon finely chopped green bell pepper

1 tablespoon chopped fresh cilantro

1 tablespoon fresh lime juice

1 teaspoon seeded, finely chopped jalapeño
  or other chili pepper, or to taste

  Pinch of salt, or to taste

1 teaspoon olive oil

2 tablespoons shredded part-skim mozzarella or
  reduced-fat Monterey Jack cheese

1. Preheat oven to 400 degrees F. Wash the potatoes thoroughly; pierce with the tip of a knife and bake directly on the oven rack until tender, about 45 minutes. Let cool.

2. Meanwhile, make the salsa: In a bowl, combine the tomato, corn, black beans, cucumber, scallion, 2 tablespoons olive oil, green pepper, cilantro, lime juice and jalapeño; add salt to taste.

3. Halve the potatoes lengthwise and, using a teaspoon, carefully remove all but ⅛ to ¼ inch of the potato, leaving the skin intact. Reserve the insides of the potatoes for another use. Brush the inside of the potato shells lightly with the 1 teaspoon olive oil. Preheat the broiler. Place the potato skins cut side up on a baking sheet and broil 3 or 4 inches from the heat 5 minutes. Turn the skins over and broil on the other side for 1 minute.

4. Spoon the salsa into the potato skins, dividing it evenly. Sprinkle with the cheese. Broil the skins just until the cheese is melted. Serve immediately.

CRISP GARLIC POTATO SKINS

Makes 4 servings

94 CALORIES PER SERVING

2 G PROTEIN

4 G FAT

14 G CARBOHYDRATE

26 MG SODIUM

1 MG CHOLESTEROL

A NUTRITIOUS, LIFE-SUSTAINING FOOD, the potato contains protein, carbohydrates, vitamins, minerals and, best of all, no fat.

With the skin, it is an excellent source of fiber. Simpler and lighter than the preceding recipe, these are a satisfying snack just the same.

2 large russet potatoes
1 tablespoon olive oil
1 garlic clove, crushed through a press
2 teaspoons grated Parmesan cheese,
   preferably Parmigiano-Reggiano
¼ teaspoon dried oregano

1. Preheat oven to 400 degrees F. Wash the potatoes thoroughly; pierce with the tip of a knife and bake directly on the oven rack until soft, about 45 minutes. Let stand until cool enough to handle.

2. Cut potatoes into lengthwise quarters and scoop out the centers, leaving ⅛ inch to ¼ inch lining the skin. Reserve the insides of the potatoes for another use.

3. Preheat the broiler. Combine the oil and garlic in a small bowl. Brush the potato skins inside and out with the oil mixture. Place skin side up on a baking sheet and broil until crisp, about 2 minutes. Turn skin side down and sprinkle inside with the Parmesan and oregano. Broil until golden brown, about 3 minutes. Cool slightly before serving.

CELERY STUFFED *with* BLUE CHEESE

Makes 12 servings

WHEN PUREED TOGETHER, skim-milk ricotta and low-fat cottage cheese become as smooth as cream cheese. The following is a light re-creation of the popular celery stuffed with blue cheese.

12   outside ribs celery, trimmed and cut into 3-inch lengths
½   cup part-skim ricotta
½   cup low-fat cottage cheese
2   ounces crumbled blue cheese
     Dash of Tabasco or other hot sauce

1. Prepare the celery and place in a bowl of ice and water. Cover and refrigerate until ready to serve.

2. In food processor, puree the ricotta and cottage cheese until smooth. Transfer to a small bowl. Add the blue cheese and Tabasco; stir until blended. Cover and refrigerate until ready to serve.

3. At serving time, drain the celery and pat dry with paper towels. Stuff each rib of celery with a rounded teaspoonful of the blue cheese mixture and arrange on a platter.

TIP

* *Serve this blue cheese mixture as a dip for raw vegetables or thin it with skim milk and use as a salad dressing.*

44 CALORIES PER SERVING
4 G PROTEIN
2 G FAT
2 G CARBOHYDRATE
152 MG SODIUM
7 MG CHOLESTEROL

Chapter 3

Soups

SOUPS

"SOUP IS CUISINE'S KINDEST COURSE," an anonymous sage once remarked, and latter-day nutritionists have since found plenty of reason to agree. In the history of my own family, soup has played a particularly soothing role. When my daughter was a toddler, she nearly exhausted my patience with her refusal to eat meat. To hamburgers, lamb chops and steak, she shook her head in an emphatic NO! signal. In desperation, I finally offered her a broth thick with grains and vegetables and watched in relief as her sips became greedy slurps. She thrived, and now, some 20 years later, scientific research is bearing out what nutritionists and Jewish mothers have been saying all along: Soup is good for us.

Given the fact that broth can be such a concentrated source of nourishment, it is somewhat surprising to discover that soup actually contains fewer calories per spoonful than most solid foods. When participants in a Pennsylvania study on weight loss ate a bowl of soup before their main meal, they consumed fewer total calories than those who skipped the soup. Over time, the soup eaters lost and kept off excess weight. Sipping a small bowl, apparently, can ward off the desire to overeat in the main and dessert courses.

As I PUTTER AWAY on Saturday mornings in the kitchen, chopping onions, cutting carrots and slicing celery, I noodle over what else to put into the pot. Will it be lentils, chicken, mushrooms or perhaps barley? Do I feel like curry? Or ginger? Because soup tends to be naturally low in fat, it's hard to go wrong.

By adhering to some simple steps—skimming the fat from broths, cooking vegetables in a minimum of oil, omitting the butter and cream and sticking with lean meat and rice, pasta and legumes—it is simple to excise any small amounts of fat that might otherwise sneak their way into the pot. When I make my own broth, I chill it overnight and lift off and discard the solidified fat. When I use canned, I always spoon off the small globules on the surface.

(Some of the new reduced-sodium canned broths are really quite tasty, incidentally.)

Instead of sautéing chopped raw vegetables in butter or oil, I stir them with about 1 table-spoon of my favorite olive oil and then cook them, covered, over very low heat. Called "sweating," this popular technique entices the natural juices out of the vegetables without covering them with more fat. If the vegetables begin to stick, I add a little chicken broth, not oil.

Although I like the taste of cream soups, I don't care for all their richness and extra fat. Unwilling to abandon them entirely, I've found a way to lighten them by substituting a pureed cooked potato thinned with low-fat milk for the cream. This technique works especially well in soups with spicy or assertive flavors like Spicy Creamy Cauliflower. Dried beans, when well cooked, also can impart a certain creamy softness to the broth.

Just before serving, I top each bowl with a zingy splash of color. For Italian Minestrone, for instance, I drizzle a tiny pool of basil puree over the surface, while vichyssoise gets a jot of pureed peas and fresh mint that enriches every sip. These last-minute flourishes make my soups one of the meal's prettiest courses as well as the most virtuous.

Basics

Classics

LEAN CHICKEN BROTH

Makes about 2 quarts

THE ONLY SECRET TO A LEAN BROTH is to chill it overnight so that all the fat will rise to the top and solidify. The next day, the solid layer of fat can be easily lifted off.

2-3	pounds chicken wings, backs and/or necks
3	quarts water
1	onion, halved
1	leafy rib celery
1	carrot, trimmed and pared
1	garlic clove, halved
1	bay leaf
1	sprig fresh parsley

1. Rinse the chicken thoroughly in two changes of water; drain. Place in a large (8-quart) saucepan.

2. Add the water, onion, celery, carrot, garlic, bay leaf and parsley. Heat over medium-high heat until the mixture begins to boil; reduce heat and skim any foam from the surface.

3. Cook the broth without boiling, uncovered, over medium-low heat until reduced by one-third and fragrant and flavorful, about 3 hours. Cool slightly.

4. Set a large fine-mesh strainer over a large bowl and strain the broth. Discard the solids. Refrigerate the broth overnight.

5. The next day, skim the solid fat from the surface and discard. Ladle the broth into 2-cup freezer containers, leaving behind the layer of cloudy broth on the bottom of the bowl. This should be discarded.

* When you buy whole chickens, freeze the wing tips, backs and necks in a Ziploc bag, adding to it until you have about 2 to 3 pounds, or enough from 5 or 6 chickens. If preferred, you can buy packages of backs and/or wings in the supermarket and use these to make broth.

* Defatted chicken broth is indispensable for anyone who wants to reduce fat. It can be used instead of butter for sautéing vegetables; when reduced, it becomes the basis for sauces; and it can replace some of the oil in salad dressings.

* Freeze in 2-cup containers.

DATA FOR HOMEMADE BROTHS IS INEXACT. RECIPES CONTAINING THESE BROTHS ARE APPROXIMATED AS FOLLOWS PER ¼ CUP: LESS THAN 10 CALORIES SMALL AMOUNTS OF PROTEIN TRACES OF FAT, CARBOHYDRATE, SODIUM AND CHOLESTEROL

LEAN BEEF BROTH

Makes about 2 quarts

DATA FOR HOMEMADE BROTHS
IS INEXACT. RECIPES CONTAINING
THESE BROTHS ARE APPROX-
IMATED AS FOLLOWS PER ¼ CUP:
LESS THAN 10 CALORIES
SMALL AMOUNTS OF PROTEIN
TRACES OF FAT, CARBOHYDRATE,
SODIUM AND CHOLESTEROL

I RARELY USE BEEF BROTH except as a first step in preparing certain soups. Make it one day ahead so all the solid fat can be skimmed from the surface. Browning the beef and vegetables first contributes a rich amber color, and the caramelized vegetables add depth of flavor.

2   1-inch slices beef shin with meat attached
     (2 to 3 pounds)
     Olive oil
1   large onion, halved
1   carrot, halved lengthwise
1   garlic clove, halved
3   quarts water
1   leafy rib celery
1   sprig fresh parsley
1   bay leaf

1. Wipe the surfaces of the meat with a dampened paper towel. Brush the bottom of a large (8-quart) saucepan with a thin film of olive oil. Heat the pan over medium-high heat until hot enough to sizzle the meat.

2. Add the meat, onion, carrot and garlic to the pan. Cook over medium to medium-high heat until well-browned on both sides. Add the water, celery, parsley and bay leaf. Heat to boiling; skim any foam from the surface with a slotted spoon.

3. Cook the broth without boiling, uncovered, over medium-low heat until reduced by one-third and fragrant and flavorful, about 3 hours. Cool slightly.

4. Set a large fine-mesh strainer over a large bowl and strain the broth. Transfer the pieces of meat to a side dish; discard the remaining solids.

5. Pick over the meat, discarding any fat and gristle. Shred the meat and reserve for soup. Refrigerate the broth overnight.

6. The next day, skim the solid fat from the surface and discard. Ladle the broth into 2-cup freezer containers, leaving behind the layer of cloudy broth on the bottom of the bowl. This should be discarded.

LEAN VEGETABLE BROTH

Makes about 2 quarts

IT IS DIFFICULT TO MAKE A TASTY BROTH without the protein and richness that is extracted from bones. Lightly browning the vegetables, however, provides the necessary flavor dimension without resorting to meat.

2	cups chopped onions
2	cups sliced carrots
1	cup diced (¼-inch) parsnips
1	leek, washed, trimmed and sliced
½	head garlic, unpeeled
2	teaspoons olive oil
2	cups chopped Savoy cabbage
1	pound spinach, rinsed (do not trim)
1	cup sliced mushrooms
1	cup sliced celery, plus a few celery leaves
1	small zucchini, trimmed and diced (¼-inch)
1	small yellow squash, trimmed and diced (¼-inch)
1	can (14½ ounces) whole tomatoes with juice
½	cup packed fresh parsley leaves
1	bay leaf
1	sprig fresh thyme, or pinch dried
3	quarts water

1. Combine the onions, carrots, parsnips, leek and garlic in a large (8-quart) saucepan; add the olive oil and stir to blend. Cook, uncovered, over medium heat, stirring often, just until the vegetables wilt and begin to turn golden, about 15 minutes. Do not overbrown.

TIPS

* *Do not add extra portions of cabbage, or the flavor will overwhelm that of the other vegetables. Savoy cabbage, which has a round head with crinkly, light green leaves, is a common supermarket item.*

* *Note that this recipe calls for ½ head of garlic, not ½ clove.*

* *When onions, carrots, parsnips and other aromatic vegetables are very lightly browned, their natural sugars caramelize from the heat of cooking. Caramelization adds depth of flavor and color to broth.*

2. Add the cabbage, spinach, mushrooms, celery, zucchini, yellow squash, tomatoes and juice, parsley, bay leaf and thyme; stir to blend. Add the water. Heat to boiling; skim any fat from the surface.

3. Cook the broth without boiling, uncovered, over medium-low heat until reduced by one-third, about 2 hours. Set a large fine-mesh strainer over a large bowl and strain the broth. Press down on solids to extract juices. Discard the solids.

4. Ladle into 2-cup freezer containers.

DATA FOR HOMEMADE BROTHS IS INEXACT. RECIPES CONTAINING THESE BROTHS ARE APPROXIMATED AS FOLLOWS PER ¼ CUP: LESS THAN 10 CALORIES SMALL AMOUNTS OF PROTEIN TRACES OF FAT, CARBOHYDRATE, SODIUM AND CHOLESTEROL

VEGETABLE CHICKEN & RICE SOUP

Makes 8 servings

TOUTED FOR ITS MEDICINAL BENEFITS, remembered for its ability to soothe and pamper, chicken soup is a bona fide classic. I keep the fat calories to a minimum by making the broth with skinless chicken breasts. Full flavor is achieved from the meaty chicken and the vegetables.

2   pounds skinless chicken breasts, split

3   quarts water

1   leafy green celery top

1   small onion, halved

1   garlic clove, crushed with the side of a knife

1   sprig fresh parsley

1   bay leaf

½   cup uncooked long-grain white rice

1   cup trimmed, sliced (¼-inch) fresh green beans

½   cup diced (¼-inch) carrot
    Salt to taste

½   cup diced (¼-inch) zucchini

½   cup diced (¼-inch) yellow squash

½   cup fresh or frozen small green peas
    Freshly ground black pepper

¼   cup packed fresh parsley leaves

1   tablespoon fresh dill and/or basil (optional)

1   teaspoon fresh thyme leaves, stripped from stems,
      or pinch dried

1   strip (½ x 2 inches) lemon zest
      (removed with a vegetable peeler)

1. Rinse the chicken in cold water and, using kitchen scissors, cut off any clumps of fat. Place in a large (6-to-8-quart) saucepan. Add the water, celery top, onion, garlic, parsley and bay leaf. Heat to boiling over high heat; reduce heat to low; skim any foam from the top of the broth.

2. Cook the broth without boiling, uncovered, over low heat, 1 hour. Transfer the cooked chicken breasts to a bowl; continue to simmer the broth. When the chicken breasts are cool enough to handle, pull the meat from the bones in large pieces; set the meat aside in the bowl. Return the bones to the broth. Ladle a small amount of the broth over the chicken meat to keep it moist; cover and refrigerate until ready to use. Continue simmering the remaining broth 1 hour. Cool slightly. Strain through a sieve into a large bowl and refrigerate the broth overnight.

3. The next day, remove any beads of fat that have solidified on the surface of the broth; discard. Return the broth to a large (4-to-6-quart) saucepan; heat to boiling. Stir in the rice, green beans, carrot and 1 teaspoon salt; cook, uncovered, over low heat, 10 minutes. Meanwhile, shred or cut the chicken into small pieces. Stir in the shredded chicken, zucchini, yellow squash and peas; cook until the rice and the vegetables are tender, about 5 minutes. Taste and add more salt, if needed, and a generous grinding of black pepper.

4. Meanwhile, finely chop the parsley, dill and/or basil, thyme and lemon zest and stir together.

5. Ladle the soup into bowls and stir a teaspoonful of chopped herb and lemon mixture into each serving.

NEW ENGLAND CLAM CHOWDER

Makes 4 servings

✳ *Russet potatoes have a high starch content and so make excellent thickeners for soups and stews. A mixture of pureed potatoes and milk can be substituted for cream in almost all soups.*

186 CALORIES PER SERVING

16 G PROTEIN

2 G FAT

25 G CARBOHYDRATE

405 MG SODIUM

34 MG CHOLESTEROL

THE APPEAL OF THIS SOUP, unfortunately, has often been the heavy cream, which was used to restore flavor as cooks turned to the convenience of canned clams or, worse yet, clam strips. This chowder puts the emphasis back where it should be: on good-quality, fresh clams. Every saline drop of their juice should be saved for the pot.

2-3	dozen Little Neck, small cherrystone or other small clams
2	cups water
1	thick slice onion
1	leafy celery top
1	garlic clove, crushed with the side of a knife
1	sprig fresh thyme
1	bay leaf
½	cup thinly sliced carrots
½	cup trimmed, sliced (¼-inch) celery
2	cups peeled, cubed (½-inch) russet potatoes
2	cups low-fat milk
½	teaspoon salt, or to taste
	Freshly ground black pepper
2	teaspoons fresh thyme leaves, stripped from stems, or ¼ teaspoon dried
1	teaspoon grated lemon zest

1. Select only clams that are tightly closed, with shells free of chips or cracks. Rinse in cold water and scrub the surfaces with a stiff brush; rinse again. If not using the clams immediately, store in the refrigerator on a platter or in a shallow pan and cover with a dampened dish cloth or paper towel.

2. Combine the water, onion slice, celery top, garlic, thyme and bay leaf in a large (6-to-8-quart) shallow saucepan or skillet with a tight-fitting lid. Heat to boiling over high heat; cover and simmer 10 minutes. Add the clams to the simmering broth. Cover and cook over high heat for 5 minutes, or until all the clams are opened. Discard any that refuse to open.

3. Using tongs or a slotted spoon, transfer the opened clams to a bowl. Place a fine-mesh strainer over another large bowl and strain the broth in which the clams were cooked into the bowl. Wipe out the saucepan and add the strained broth to the pan. Add the sliced carrots and sliced celery; cook in the broth just until crisp-tender, about 5 minutes; reserve, off the heat, in the broth.

4. Meanwhile, cook the potatoes in boiling salted water until tender, about 10 minutes; drain. Combine 1 cup of the cooked potatoes and 1 cup of the milk in the bowl of a food processor; process until pureed. Stir into the broth and vegetable mixture.

5. Remove the clams from their shells and chop into ¼-inch pieces. Stir into the broth mixture along with any juices. Add the remaining 1 cup cooked potatoes and gradually stir in the remaining milk until the chowder is the desired consistency.

6. Heat gently over low heat; do not boil, or the chowder may curdle. Season with salt and a generous grinding of black pepper. Mix the thyme and lemon zest together. Ladle the chowder into bowls and sprinkle each with the thyme and lemon mixture.

No-Cream Shrimp Bisque

Makes 4 servings

UNLIKE THE USUAL VERSION, which is synonymous with heavy cream and egg yolks, this shrimp bisque is based on milk that has been thickened with cornstarch.

1½	pounds medium or large shrimp, shelled and deveined (reserve the shells)
2	teaspoons olive oil
¼	cup chopped onion
1	garlic clove, crushed with the side of a knife
1	bay leaf
½	cup dry white wine
2	cups water
1	tablespoon tomato paste
3	cups low-fat or regular milk
2	tablespoons cornstarch
1	teaspoon fresh lemon juice
½	teaspoon salt, or to taste
½	teaspoon paprika plus more for garnish
	Dash of Tabasco or other hot sauce
	Freshly ground black pepper

1. Rinse the shells thoroughly with cold water; drain and reserve. Chop the shrimp; refrigerate and reserve.

TIP

✳ *Sautéing the empty shrimp shells in oil, boiling them with wine, then pureeing them in a food processor intensifies the flavor of the seafood, an imperative in low-fat dishes.*

207 CALORIES PER SERVING

20 G PROTEIN

5 G FAT

15 G CARBOHYDRATE

547 MG SODIUM

138 MG CHOLESTEROL

2. Heat the olive oil in a large (10-to-12-inch) skillet. Stir in the shrimp shells, onion, garlic and bay leaf; cook, stirring, over medium heat for 5 minutes. Stir in the wine and boil over high heat until reduced by two-thirds. Add the water and tomato paste; heat to boiling and cook, covered, 15 minutes.

3. Transfer to a food processor and process 30 seconds. Set a sieve over a large (4-quart) saucepan and strain the shrimp essence; discard the solids.

4. In a small bowl, whisk ½ cup of the milk with the cornstarch until smooth. Stir the remaining 2½ cups milk and the cornstarch mixture into the saucepan. Heat, stirring, over low heat, until the mixture begins to thicken. Do not boil. Stir in the chopped shrimp. Cook over low heat, stirring, until the shrimp are cooked through, about 5 minutes. Add the remaining ingredients. Taste and correct seasoning.

5. To serve, ladle the bisque into bowls, distributing the shrimp evenly. Sprinkle a little extra paprika on top, if desired.

CREAMY TOMATO SOUP

Makes 8 cups or 4 servings

SOUPS THICKENED WITH PUREED COOKED POTATO and enriched with low-fat milk approximate the body and texture of pureed soups thickened with heavy cream.

1 cup peeled, cubed (½-inch) russet potatoes

½ cup chopped onion

2 tablespoons water

1 teaspoon olive oil

½ teaspoon finely chopped garlic

2 cans (28 ounces each) imported Italian plum tomatoes

1 bay leaf

1 leafy sprig fresh basil

2 cups low-fat milk

1 teaspoon sugar

½ teaspoon salt, or to taste

Freshly ground black pepper

Basil & Yogurt Puree

½ cup coarsely chopped fresh basil leaves, packed

½ cup low-fat or nonfat plain yogurt

1. Combine the potato, onion, water, olive oil and garlic in a large (4-quart) saucepan. Cook, covered, over medium-low heat for 10 minutes, or until the potatoes and onions are tender.

2. Stir in the tomatoes, bay leaf and basil. Cook, covered, for 20 minutes. Cool slightly; remove the bay leaf and basil. Transfer in batches to the bowl of a food processor and puree until smooth. Place a large strainer over the saucepan and gradually press the puree through the strainer. Discard the tomato seeds.

3. Gradually whisk the milk into the tomato puree. Add sugar and salt to taste and a generous grinding of black pepper. Heat gently over low heat, stirring, until steaming hot; do not boil.

4. **Making the puree:** Chop the basil leaves finely and stir them into the yogurt in a small bowl.

5. Ladle the soup into bowls and swirl a spoonful of the basil puree into each bowl.

VICHYSSOISE *with* GREEN PEA PUREE

Makes 5 cups or 4 servings

VICHYSSOISE, FIRST SERVED AT THE RITZ in New York City in 1910, was a bland but silken soup of potato and leeks pureed with chicken broth and heavy cream. Here, potatoes and leeks provide smooth texture, and a graceful swirl of bright green pureed peas and mint brightens the flavor. An elegance worthy of the Ritz lives on.

TIP

✳ *The last-minute addition of fresh herbs and vegetable puree creates a burst of flavor that more than makes up for the loss of butter and cream. It's a useful technique to know when making all kinds of soups.*

204 CALORIES PER SERVING

9 G PROTEIN

5 G FAT

31 G CARBOHYDRATE

701 MG SODIUM

6 MG CHOLESTEROL

2   small or 1 large leek (about 12 ounces total), trimmed, halved lengthwise and rinsed thoroughly, coarsely chopped (about 1¾ cups)

1   garlic clove, crushed through a press

1   tablespoon olive oil

2   cups peeled, cubed (½-inch) russet potatoes

1   cup reduced-sodium or homemade chicken broth (page 75)

2   cups low-fat milk

1   teaspoon salt

⅛   teaspoon cayenne

     Pinch of nutmeg (optional)

Green Pea Puree

1   cup fresh or frozen small green peas

½   cup reduced-sodium or homemade chicken broth (page 75)

¼   cup low-fat milk, or more as needed

2   tablespoons chopped fresh mint leaves

1   teaspoon fresh lime juice

     Pinch of salt

     Pinch of cayenne

1   tablespoon thinly sliced fresh mint leaves for garnish

1. Combine the leek, garlic and olive oil in a large (4-quart) saucepan. Cook, stirring, over low heat, 5 minutes. Add the potatoes and chicken broth and heat to boiling. Cook, covered, over medium-low heat until the potatoes and leeks are very tender, about 10 minutes. Cool slightly.

2. Transfer to the bowl of a food processor. Puree the mixture; slowly add the milk through the feed tube and puree until the mixture is very smooth. Transfer to a large bowl. Add the salt, cayenne and nutmeg, if using. Refrigerate until chilled, about 3 hours, or less if mixture is chilled in the freezer.

3. **Making the puree:** Cook the peas and chicken broth, covered, in a small saucepan over low heat until very tender, about 15 minutes. Transfer to a blender; add the milk and mint. Blend on high speed until the mixture is very smooth. Add the lime juice, salt and cayenne. Transfer to a small bowl; refrigerate until chilled.

4. Before serving, add more milk to thin the soup if desired. Taste the chilled soup and add more salt and pepper to taste. Ladle the soup into four large soup bowls; swirl or otherwise decorate the soup with the green pea puree. Scatter the mint leaves on top.

ITALIAN MINESTRONE

Makes 6 to 8 servings

TIPS

TRADITIONAL MINESTRONE, or Italian vegetable soup, is a classic example of a hearty but healthful soup. At its best, it is filled with complex carbohydrates and is relatively low in fat. In this version, lean chicken, beef or vegetable broth forms the base. Add as many or as few vegetables as you choose. Use elbow macaroni, ditalini, orzo (a small rice-shaped pasta) or tiny shells. Use lima beans or cannellini beans or a combination.

TIPS

* *The combination of grain (pasta) and legumes in the form of lima or cannellini beans gives this soup a full component of complete protein.*

* *This soup freezes very well, so make a double batch and freeze half.*

* *The vegetables are first "sautéed" in water instead of in olive oil; but a swirl of fresh basil puree adds delicious flavor to the finished soup.*

1	cup coarsely chopped onion
½	cup coarsely chopped carrot
½	cup coarsely chopped celery
1	teaspoon finely chopped garlic
2	tablespoons water
8	cups reduced-sodium or homemade chicken, beef or vegetable broth (pages 75, 76, 78)
½	cup ditalini, small elbows or other small tubular pasta
1	teaspoon salt, or to taste
	Freshly ground black pepper to taste
2	cups rinsed, trimmed, coarsely chopped Swiss chard or escarole, packed
1	cup fresh or frozen small lima beans or cooked dried, or rinsed canned cannellini beans
1	cup trimmed and sliced (½-inch) green beans
½	cup trimmed and diced (¼-inch) zucchini
½	cup fresh or frozen small peas
½	cup peeled, seeded and diced fresh or canned tomatoes
¼	cup finely chopped fresh basil or fresh Italian (flat-leaf) parsley
1	tablespoon olive oil

1. Combine the onion, carrot, celery, garlic and water in a large (4-to-5-quart) saucepan. Cover and cook over low heat 10 minutes, stirring occasionally, until the vegetables are tender. Add the broth and heat to boiling.

2. Stir in the pasta, salt and freshly ground pepper; cook, stirring, over medium heat, 5 minutes. Add the Swiss chard or escarole, lima or cannellini beans and green beans; cook, uncovered, for 20 minutes, or until the vegetables and pasta are very tender.

3. Add the zucchini, peas and tomatoes; cook 10 minutes. Add salt and pepper to taste.

4. Whisk the basil or parsley and oil together in a small bowl.

5. Ladle the soup into bowls. Swirl ½ teaspoon of the basil oil into each bowl of soup.

148 CALORIES PER SERVING

8 G PROTEIN

4 G FAT

22 G CARBOHYDRATE

480 MG SODIUM

1 MG CHOLESTEROL

CREAMY SWEET CORN CHOWDER

Makes 4 servings

TIP

❋ *When reducing fat in a favorite recipe, you can often use a small amount of a high-fat food as a garnish, as with the bacon in this recipe.*

234 CALORIES PER SERVING

9 G PROTEIN

7 G FAT

39 G CARBOHYDRATE

173 MG SODIUM

14 MG CHOLESTEROL

THE STARCH FROM THE CORN and the potatoes brings a creamy texture—without the cream. Save this recipe for the height of the season, when the corn is sweet and tender. Inevitably, there are a few rainy days in August and September when a bowl of steaming chowder is welcome. Add just a hint of bacon flavor—and a minimum of saturated fat—by sprinkling the soup with a fine crumble of one slice of crisp, smoky bacon.

1	tablespoon unsalted butter or vegetable oil
½	cup finely chopped onion
2½	cups fresh corn kernels, cut from cobs (about 5 ears)
1	cup peeled, diced russet potatoes
2	cups reduced-sodium or homemade chicken broth (page 75)
1	bay leaf
1½	cups low-fat milk

Spicy Tomato Puree

1	thin slice lean bacon
½	cup chopped ripe tomato
1	teaspoon chili powder
⅛	teaspoon cayenne, or more to taste

1. Heat the butter or oil in a large (4-quart) saucepan until melted. Add the onion and cook, stirring, over medium-low heat, until tender, about 5 minutes.

2. Add 2 cups of the corn kernels (reserve the remaining ½ cup), the potatoes, broth and bay leaf. Cover and cook over low heat until tender, about 15 minutes. Remove the bay leaf. Cool slightly; puree in a food processor, in batches if necessary. Press the pureed mixture through a sieve set over the saucepan. Add the milk and the remaining ½ cup corn kernels to the saucepan. Heat over low heat, stirring; do not boil.

3. **Making the puree:** Meanwhile, cook the bacon in a medium (8-to-10-inch) non-stick skillet; drain the bacon on a paper towel; chop very fine; set aside. Wipe out the skillet and add the tomato, chili powder and cayenne. Heat, stirring, until the tomato cooks to a thick puree, about 3 minutes.

4. To serve, ladle the soup into large shallow bowls. Place a spoonful of the tomato puree in the center of each and sprinkle lightly with the bacon, dividing evenly among the bowls.

MUSHROOM & BARLEY SOUP

Makes 5 cups or 4 servings

TYPICALLY, THIS SOUP IS BASED ON A MEAT BROTH that can be fatty. But cooked mushrooms are so "meaty"-tasting that they can become a meat substitute. Soy sauce adds a toasty flavor to this all-vegetable soup.

2 packages (10 ounces each) white button mushrooms, wiped clean
1 cup chopped onion
2 teaspoons vegetable oil
2 garlic cloves, finely chopped
½ cup diced carrots
1 cup diced celery
1 bay leaf
1 tablespoon chopped fresh thyme leaves, stripped from stems, or 1 teaspoon dried
4 cups water
⅓ cup pearl barley
2 tablespoons reduced-sodium soy sauce
½ teaspoon salt

Mushroom & Red Bell Pepper Garnish

1 teaspoon olive oil
2 tablespoons finely diced red bell pepper
¼ teaspoon minced garlic
Salt to taste
Freshly ground black pepper to taste

1 cup washed, chopped packed spinach, watercress or arugula

TIPS

❋ There is a lot more to mushrooms than meets the eye— or the palate. In the Orient, they are revered in folklore as a curative. Western scientists continue to look at these unassuming fungi, especially the shiitake, for evidence of medicinal qualities. Meanwhile, they are a fat-free, sodium-free, tasty source of fiber.

❋ For more on barley, see the note for Barley Tabbouleh, page 112.

❋ Reduced-sodium soy sauce has half to two-thirds less sodium than regular soy sauce does, and many people prefer its less salty taste. Taken together, mushrooms and soy give a rich, meaty flavor to gravies, soups and stews.

1. Select 4 large mushrooms; slice thin and set aside for the garnish. Coarsely chop the remaining mushrooms into ¼-inch pieces (approximately 5 cups). Set aside.

2. Combine the onion and oil in a large (4-quart) saucepan. Cook, stirring, over medium-low heat, until tender, about 5 minutes. Stir in the garlic, carrots, celery, bay leaf and thyme. Cover and cook over low heat, until the vegetables are very tender but not browned, about 15 minutes.

3. Stir in the chopped mushrooms; cook, uncovered, stirring, over medium heat until the mushrooms give out their liquid. Add the water, barley, soy sauce and salt. Stir over high heat until boiling; reduce heat to low. Cover and cook until the barley is tender, about 45 minutes. Remove the bay leaf.

4. **Meanwhile, prepare the garnish:** In a medium (8-to-10-inch) nonstick skillet, heat the oil. Add the reserved sliced mushrooms and red pepper and cook, stirring, over medium-low heat, until tender, about 5 minutes. Add the garlic; cook, stirring, until blended. Season with salt and pepper. Set aside.

5. Add the spinach, watercress or arugula to the soup. Simmer until tender, about 5 minutes. Taste the soup and add salt and a grinding of black pepper, if needed. Ladle into bowls and top with the garnish.

164 CALORIES PER SERVING

7 G PROTEIN

4 G FAT

28 G CARBOHYDRATE

586 MG SODIUM

0 MG CHOLESTEROL

LENTIL & BROWN RICE SOUP

Makes 6 to 8 servings

TIPS

* *If bean cookery is new for you, lentils are a good place to begin. They require no soaking and will cook to tenderness in less than 30 minutes, making them a very convenient choice.*

* *You can further reduce the fat calories by omitting the oil in step 1 and adding a little water to the vegetables, as needed, to keep the mixture moist.*

AT EVERY TURN, we are encouraged to add more grains and legumes to our diet. The truth is, there are few classic bean and grain dishes in our repertoire. In this soup, a favorite of my family, the proteins in the lentils and the rice join forces to make a hearty and satisfying main dish. Brown rice is nutritious and flavorful because none of the nutrients and fiber—or the wonderful nutty taste—in the bran layer have been stripped away. This hearty soup is marbled with fresh spinach and garnished with sautéed red bell pepper.

1½	cups chopped onion
2	teaspoons olive oil or water
1	cup sliced carrots
1	teaspoon finely chopped garlic
1	tablespoon water
1	tablespoon curry powder
1	teaspoon ground coriander
8	cups water
1½	cups dried brown lentils, rinsed and sorted
1	bay leaf
¼	cup long-grain brown rice
1	teaspoon salt, or more to taste
2	cups rinsed, trimmed, packed fresh spinach leaves
	Freshly ground black pepper

Red Bell Pepper Garnish

2	teaspoons vegetable oil
½	cup diced red bell pepper
2	tablespoons finely chopped fresh Italian (flat-leaf) parsley

**1 small garlic clove, crushed through a press
   Freshly ground black pepper**

1. Combine the onion and olive oil or water in a large (4-to-6-quart) saucepan. Heat over low heat, stirring, until the onion is tender, about 5 minutes. Add the carrots, garlic and 1 tablespoon water; stir to blend. Cover and cook over low heat until the onion is golden, about 5 minutes. Uncover and stir in the curry powder and coriander. Cook, stirring, 1 minute.

2. Add the 8 cups water, lentils and bay leaf. Heat to boiling over high heat. Reduce heat to low and cook, stirring, occasionally, until the lentils are tender, about 45 minutes. Stir in the rice and salt; cook, uncovered, stirring occasionally, until the rice is tender and the soup is thickened, about 45 minutes. Add small amounts of water to the soup if it becomes too thick. Remove the bay leaf. Stir in the spinach and cook, stirring, until wilted, about 5 minutes. Season to taste with more salt and a grinding of black pepper.

3. **Making the garnish:** Meanwhile, heat the 2 teaspoons oil in a small (8-inch) non-stick skillet; add the red bell pepper and cook, stirring, over medium heat, until the edges begin to brown, about 5 minutes. Add the parsley and garlic and cook 1 minute. Remove from the heat. Season with a grinding of black pepper.

4. Ladle into bowls and top with the garnish.

264 CALORIES PER SERVING

16 G PROTEIN

4 G FAT

44 G CARBOHYDRATE

388 MG SODIUM

0 MG CHOLESTEROL

Spicy Creamy Cauliflower Soup

Makes 4 servings

TIP

✳ *To reduce the fat, use chicken broth for part of the vegetable oil.*

167 CALORIES PER SERVING

8 G PROTEIN

5 G FAT

25 G CARBOHYDRATE

631 MG SODIUM

3 MG CHOLESTEROL

SPICY INDIAN-INSPIRED FLAVORS of curry, ginger and turmeric, together with the sweetness of apple, heighten the flavor of this soup. Serve hot or chilled.

1	tablespoon vegetable oil
½	cup chopped onion
1	teaspoon peeled, grated fresh gingerroot
1½	teaspoons curry powder
½	teaspoon turmeric
3	cups chopped cauliflower (small pieces)
½	cup peeled, cored and chopped Granny Smith apple
2	cups reduced-sodium or homemade chicken broth (page 75)
1	cup peeled, thinly sliced russet potatoes
1	teaspoon salt
1	cup low-fat milk

Tomato-Mint Garnish

¼	cup diced tomato
1	teaspoon chopped fresh mint
¼	teaspoon peeled, grated gingerroot

1. Heat the oil in a large (4-quart) saucepan over medium-low heat. Add the onion and cook, stirring frequently, until soft, about 3 minutes. Lower heat, add the ginger, curry powder and turmeric and continue cooking for another 2 minutes.

2. Add the cauliflower, apple, broth and potatoes to the onion mixture; stir and heat to boiling. Cover and cook over low heat until the potatoes are tender, about 15 minutes.

3. Add the salt and cool to room temperature. When cool, combine the cauliflower mixture and the milk in a blender and blend until smooth.

4. **Making the garnish:** In a small bowl, stir together the tomato flesh, mint and ginger. Set aside.

5. Return the soup to the saucepan and heat over low heat just until warm. Do not boil. Ladle into serving bowls and garnish with the tomato-mint mixture.

Chapter 4

SALADS & DRESSINGS

SALADS & DRESSINGS

I GREW UP IN A SALAD-EATING family. Each night, after the main course, my mother served a rough mixture of bitter greens—it was almost always chicory—with a sharp red-wine vinegar. I picked away at it, wishing the greens weren't so biting and hoping my mother wouldn't notice that I wasn't eating (she always did), while my brother, sister and father dipped makeshift croutons of torn crusty bread into the heady vinaigrette and devoured forkfuls of salad.

Mother kept her dressing in a pint-sized Ball jar in the kitchen cabinet over the stove. Before she shook it, the top layer was winy red and three times as thick as the olive oil below. It was peppered with flecks of oregano, used sparingly, "because too much can make a dish bitter." Floating in it was a whole clove of garlic that had been pierced with a toothpick, presumably so its juices could be released into the dressing but also so it could be retrieved easily if it somehow found its way into the bowl

when the salad was being mixed.

For my mother, making a dressing that was composed of more acid than oil was a matter of instinct and taste rather than a conscious decision to reduce fat intake. Somewhere between childhood and adulthood, however, I reversed my mother's formula and began using three times more oil (fat) than lemon juice. Having Americanized and enriched the old recipes, I now find myself making my way back, reformulating my dressings to be more like hers.

HIGH IN FIBER, vitamins and minerals, salads are supposed to be the ultimate food for good health, but in reality, they usually aren't. Most of the time, the fault lies in the dressing, which generally contains too much fat: mayonnaise enveloping potato, egg, cabbage and tuna salads; sour cream stifling cucumbers; creamy blue cheese loading down iceberg lettuce.

Fortunately, remedies abound. Fat-reduced

and nonfat mayonnaise are wonderful inventions. Yogurt, pureed cottage cheese whirred with low-fat milk in a blender, and buttermilk are all tasty solutions to the creamy dilemma. Using the sweet juice of a diced tomato and lots of fresh herbs to coat the lettuce leaves makes a tasty "dressing," especially when locally grown vine-ripened tomatoes are in season. Using chicken broth in place of some of the oil is another way to add fullness of flavor. And, of course, simply reversing the three-to-one ratio of oil to acid is a brilliant strategy, and one that my mother will be quite surprised to learn is "new."

CUCUMBER SALAD *with* BUTTERMILK, YOGURT & DILL DRESSING

Makes 4 servings

TRADITIONAL CUCUMBER SALADS are tossed with sour cream. The textures of the creamy dressing and crunchy vegetables are left intact, but the creamy consistency now comes from nonfat buttermilk. Originally, buttermilk was the nearly fatless liquid left after the cream was churned into butter. Today it is made commercially by adding special bacteria to nonfat or low-fat milk to make it thick and tangy. It's a good substitute for sour cream in dressings and dips.

48 CALORIES PER SERVING
3 G PROTEIN
1 G FAT
8 G CARBOHYDRATE
190 MG SODIUM
3 MG CHOLESTEROL

½ cup buttermilk
½ cup low-fat plain yogurt
3 tablespoons chopped fresh dill
1 teaspoon cider vinegar
½ teaspoon sugar
1 seedless cucumber, thinly sliced (about 2 cups)
¼ cup chopped red onion
2 tablespoons finely diced carrot
1 garlic clove, finely chopped
½ teaspoon freshly ground black pepper, or to taste
¼ teaspoon salt, or to taste
   Fresh dill sprigs for garnish

1. In a medium bowl, stir together the buttermilk, yogurt, dill, vinegar and sugar.

2. Add the cucumber, onion, carrot, garlic, pepper and salt; stir to blend.

3. Serve chilled, garnished with sprigs of dill.

TOSSED GREEN WALDORF SALAD

Makes 4 servings (1½ cups per serving)

Although the traditional Waldorf salad of chopped apples, celery and walnuts is bound with fat-laden mayonnaise, the other ingredients are inherently healthful. To lighten this familiar classic, I substituted a tangy dressing of vegetable oil, lemon juice and lemon zest, with a jot of walnut oil to reinforce the toasted walnut flavor. Three types of apples—Granny Smiths, Yellow Delicious and Red Delicious—add excitement. Serve on a snappy mixture of greens and garnish with warm toasted walnuts.

4-6	whole salad leaves (radicchio, red leaf, romaine), rinsed and trimmed

Dressing

2	tablespoons vegetable oil
2	tablespoons fresh lemon juice
2	teaspoons walnut oil
1	teaspoon grated lemon zest
1	Granny Smith apple, unpeeled, cored, quartered and cut into thin wedges
1	Yellow Delicious apple, unpeeled, cored, quartered and cut into thin wedges
1	Red Delicious apple, unpeeled, cored, quartered and cut into thin wedges
3	darker green outside ribs of celery, rinsed, trimmed and cut into thin slices (about 1½ cups)
2	tablespoons coarsely chopped light green inside celery leaves
2	tablespoons coarsely chopped fresh dill
¼	cup coarsely broken walnuts

TIP

* *Walnut oil adds a special measure of flavor and is well worth obtaining for this recipe alone. It is available in gourmet or health-food stores. If it is to be stored long, it should be kept in the refrigerator to prevent it from becoming rancid.*

203 CALORIES PER SERVING

3 G PROTEIN

14 G FAT

20 G CARBOHYDRATE

46 MG SODIUM

0 MG CHOLESTEROL

1. Wrap the salad leaves in a dish towel and refrigerate until ready to use.

2. Making the dressing: Place the oil, lemon juice, walnut oil and grated lemon zest in a large bowl; whisk to blend. As the apples are sliced, add them to the dressing and toss to coat, to prevent darkening. Add the celery, celery leaves and dill to the dressing. Toss to blend.

3. Divide the salad greens among four salad plates. Top each with a mound of the apple salad.

4. Place the walnuts in a small skillet set over medium-low heat and stir constantly until the nuts are warm and glistening. Divide evenly over the salads.

SEVEN BEAN SALAD *with* LEMON & MUSTARD DRESSING

Makes 8 cups or 8 servings

199 CALORIES PER SERVING

9 G PROTEIN

6 G FAT

29 G CARBOHYDRATE

286 MG SODIUM

0 MG CHOLESTEROL

THIS RECIPE IS A CONTEMPORARY VERSION of the Three Bean Salad of church suppers and family picnics. It contains less oil than the traditional version, and the bean selection has been expanded to provide even more of the complex carbohydrates than usual.

1   cup trimmed, cut (1-inch pieces) fresh green beans

1   cup trimmed, cut (1-inch pieces) fresh wax beans

1   cup cooked dried or rinsed canned red kidney beans

1   cup cooked dried or rinsed canned cannellini
     (white kidney) beans

1   cup cooked dried or rinsed canned black beans

1   cup cooked dried or rinsed canned chick-peas

1   cup cooked frozen or fresh lima beans

½   cup chopped sweet white onion

½   cup thinly sliced green scallion tops

¼   cup finely chopped fresh Italian (flat-leaf) parsley

Lemon & Mustard Dressing

3   tablespoons olive oil

1   teaspoon grainy Dijon-style mustard

2   tablespoons fresh lemon juice

½   teaspoon grated lemon zest

¼   teaspoon salt, or to taste

Freshly ground black pepper to taste

1. Cook the green beans and the wax beans in a medium (3-quart) saucepan of boiling salted water, uncovered, until tender, 5 to 8 minutes. Drain and rinse with cold running water. Set aside.

2. In a large bowl, combine the green beans, wax beans, red kidney beans, cannellini beans, black beans, chick-peas, lima beans, onion, scallion tops and parsley.

3. **Making the dressing:** In a separate bowl, whisk together the oil, mustard, lemon juice, lemon zest, salt and pepper. Pour over the bean mixture and toss gently.

4. Let the salad stand for 1 hour before serving to allow the flavors to blend.

MACARONI &
SEVEN BEAN SALAD

Makes 10 cups or 8 servings as a main course

2   cups cooked elbow macaroni (1 cup uncooked), cooled
    Seven Bean Salad (opposite page)
    Double recipe of Lemon & Mustard Dressing
      (opposite page)

282 CALORIES PER SERVING

10 G PROTEIN

11 G FAT

37 G CARBOHYDRATE

361 MG SODIUM

0 MG CHOLESTEROL

Add the macaroni to the Seven Bean Salad and toss with a double recipe of the Lemon & Mustard Dressing.

RED CABBAGE & PEPPER SLAW

Makes 4 servings

85 CALORIES PER SERVING

1 G PROTEIN

7 G FAT

6 G CARBOHYDRATE

158 MG SODIUM

0 MG CHOLESTEROL

CLASSIC COLESLAW CAN BE MADE with heavy cream, mayonnaise or an oil-and-vinegar combination. The oil-and-vinegar dressed slaws, with their unsaturated oils, are preferred by the health-conscious over mayonnaise or cream-based slaws. In this recipe, red cabbage mixes with yellow bell peppers for a strikingly zesty combination.

1   pound red cabbage, cored, sliced in ⅓-inch strips (about 4 cups)

1   yellow bell pepper, seeds, stem and white ribs removed, cut in ⅓-inch strips (about 1 cup)

1   tablespoon white-wine vinegar

1   teaspoon prepared Dijon-style mustard

¼   teaspoon salt

¼   teaspoon freshly ground black pepper

2   tablespoons extra-virgin olive oil

⅛   cup green scallion tops, cut into fine slivers

1. Combine the cabbage and yellow pepper in a large bowl. Set aside.

2. In a separate bowl, whisk together the vinegar, mustard, salt and pepper. Continue whisking vigorously while gradually adding the oil in a thin stream.

3. Add the dressing to the cabbage mixture and toss to blend. Refrigerate, covered, at least 1 hour before serving. Garnish with the scallion tops and serve.

SHREDDED CARROT SALAD

Makes 4 servings

I ALWAYS LOVED THE SHREDDED CARROT in this salad, but I never understood the reason for the raisins and mayonnaise that were part of it in my grade-school cafeteria. Here, the carrots are still shredded, but the flavors are light with lime juice and spicily intriguing with cilantro and jalapeño peppers. The dressing replaces mayonnaise with olive oil.

4	cups coarsely shredded carrots
2	tablespoons chopped fresh cilantro
1½	teaspoons ground cumin
2	tablespoons fresh lime juice
2	teaspoons seeded and finely chopped jalapeño peppers
2	tablespoons vegetable oil
½	teaspoon salt, or more to taste

1. Combine the carrots and cilantro in a medium bowl.

2. In a small (6-to-8-inch) skillet, heat the cumin over very low heat until warm and fragrant, about 1 minute. Stir in the lime juice, jalapeño, oil and salt until blended.

3. Pour the dressing over the carrot and cilantro mixture. Toss well.

TIP

✳ *Carrot contain lots of beta carotene—a substance that has recently been recognized for its role in cancer prevention. One raw carrot has about 30 calories and supplies more than the recommended daily dietary allowance of vitamin A.*

II3 CALORIES PER SERVING

I G PROTEIN

7 G FAT

I2 G CARBOHYDRATE

307 MG SODIUM

0 MG CHOLESTEROL

BARLEY TABBOULEH

Makes 6 serving

TIPS

✳ *Barley, like rice, is refined (polished) to make it white. Polished or pearl barley does lose some of its natural protein, fiber and B vitamins when the outside or bran layer is polished off. But even polished (pearl) barley is nutritious. A cup of cooked barley supplies respectable amounts of potassium and B vitamins. Dry barley expands to four times its original measurement after it is cooked. Pearl barley cooks in about 45 minutes.*

✳ *For a note on Kirby cucumbers, see page 52.*

164 CALORIES PER SERVING

4 G PROTEIN

7 G FAT

22 G CARBOHYDRATE

250 MG SODIUM

0 MG CHOLESTEROL

TABBOULEH IS A MIDDLE EASTERN DISH made with cracked wheat berries (also called bulgur) and lots of parsley, mint and lemon juice. In this version, pearl barley, a more readily available grain, is used. Found in every supermarket in either a plastic bag (usually displayed with the dried beans) or in a 1-pound box (the label often simply says barley, not pearl barley), it has been neglected in every-day cooking and is usually reserved for the soup pot.

¾	cup pearl barley
1	cup diced (¼-inch) tomato
1	cup peeled, diced (¼-inch) seedless or Kirby cucumber
½	cup diced (¼-inch) green bell pepper
½	cup red onion
1	cup thin (⅛-inch) crosswise slices of the inside leaves of romaine lettuce
½	cup finely chopped fresh Italian (flat-leaf) parsley
¼	cup finely chopped fresh mint
3	tablespoons extra-virgin olive oil
2	tablespoons fresh lemon juice
1	garlic clove, crushed through a press
½	teaspoon salt, or to taste
	Freshly ground black pepper to taste

1. Cook the barley in plenty of boiling water until tender, about 45 minutes. Drain and rinse with cold water; cool.

2. Combine the barley, tomato, cucumber, green pepper, red onion, romaine lettuce, parsley and mint in a large bowl.

3. In a separate bowl, mix together the olive oil, lemon juice, garlic, salt and pepper. Pour over the barley mixture and toss gently.

4. Let the salad stand for 1 hour to allow the flavors to blend. For best flavor, serve immediately.

ROAST POTATO SALAD

Makes 4 servings

I ADORE THE TASTE AND TEXTURE of roast potatoes. This simple salad of crisp, oven-roasted new potatoes is tossed with onion and red bell pepper and served over a bed of arugula or other greens. Serve it with other salads as part of a vegetarian menu or with roast chicken.

2	pounds small new (red-skinned) red potatoes, halved, or quartered if large
2	tablespoons extra-virgin olive oil
1	tablespoon fresh thyme leaves, or several pinches dried
1	green bell pepper, cut in ½-inch-wide strips
1	medium-size sweet white onion, cut in ½-inch-wide wedges
¼	cup slivered (⅛-x-1-inch) red bell pepper
2	tablespoons white-wine vinegar
½	teaspoon salt, or to taste
¼	teaspoon freshly ground black pepper, or to taste
1	bunch arugula, rinsed and trimmed, or other greens, such as watercress or small, tender spinach leaves.

1. Preheat oven to 400 degrees F.

2. Toss the potatoes with 1 tablespoon of the oil and 1 teaspoon of the fresh thyme or a pinch dried. Place in a single layer in a large roasting pan or two smaller pans and roast 15 minutes.

3. Meanwhile, combine the green pepper, onion, remaining olive oil and 1 teaspoon of the fresh thyme or a pinch dried in a medium bowl; toss to blend. When the potatoes have roasted for 15 minutes, add the onion and pepper mixture to the pan or pans. Loosen the potatoes from the pan with a metal spatula and stir the mixture. Roast the potatoes and vegetables, turning the potatoes occasionally so they will brown evenly, until the potatoes are tender and the onion begins to darken and caramelize at the edges, about 45 minutes more.

4. Cool slightly in roasting pan. Meanwhile, combine the remaining 1 teaspoon fresh thyme or a pinch dried, red pepper, vinegar, salt and pepper in a large bowl; add the roast potato mixture; toss to blend. Serve warm or at room temperature on arugula or other greens.

SWEET POTATO SALAD

Makes 4 servings

TIPS

✳ *If using dried sage, chop it along with the parsley to rehydrate it and bring out its flavor.*

✳ *Bake sweet potatoes at 400 degrees F until tender when pierced with a fork, 45 to 55 minutes. Do not overbake; they should not be mushy.*

✳ *The dried currants reinforce the sweetness of the sweet potatoes. What are commonly known as dried currants are actually not currant berries at all but the dried fruit of the black Corinth (Zante) grape.*

142 CALORIES PER SERVING

2 G PROTEIN

7 G FAT

20 G CARBOHYDRATE

179 MG SODIUM

0 MG CHOLESTEROL

MY MOTHER-IN-LAW makes her potato salad with cut-up boiled potatoes tossed with mayonnaise, hard-boiled eggs and chopped pickles. Sweet potatoes, although higher in calories than ordinary potatoes, have all the same nutritional virtues: they contain hardly a trace of fat and are one of the most nutrient-dense of all vegetables. Half a cup of mashed sweet potatoes has four times the recommended daily allowance of vitamin A and only 103 calories. The following recipe takes the classic formula for a potato salad with lemon and oil dressing and adds a little sage and plenty of crunchy celery to counter the soft texture of the "sweets."

2   baked sweet potatoes, peeled, halved lengthwise and sliced
     into ¼-inch-thick semicircles (about 4 cups)
1½ cups thin diagonal slices celery
½   cup thinly sliced red onion
1   tablespoon chopped fresh Italian (flat-leaf) parsley
1   teaspoon minced fresh sage leaves, or ½ teaspoon
     crumbled dried
1   tablespoon dried currants, soaked in hot water for 5 minutes
2   tablespoons fresh lemon juice
2   tablespoons extra-virgin olive oil
¼   teaspoon salt, or to taste

1. Combine the sweet potatoes, celery, onion, parsley and sage in a large bowl. Drain the currants and add to the bowl.

2. In a small bowl or cup, whisk the lemon juice, olive oil and salt until blended.

3. Add the dressing to the sweet potato mixture and gently toss to blend.

TUNA SALAD *with* GREEN BEANS & TOMATOES

Makes 2 servings as a main course or 4 servings as an appetizer

REDUCING THE MAYONNAISE is the first step to creating a more healthful version of tuna salad. Adding textures, colors and flavors is the second. Here, a vinaigrette dressing moistens the tuna, while the vegetables provide crunch.

467 CALORIES PER MAIN-COURSE SERVING

52 G PROTEIN

19 G FAT

25 G CARBOHYDRATE

774 MG SODIUM

73 MG CHOLESTEROL

2   cups trimmed, cut (1-inch lengths) green beans
2   cans (6½-ounces each) solid white, water-packed tuna,
      drained well
2   cups ¼-inch-thick wedges seeded plum tomatoes
1   cup thin lengthwise slices red onion
1   tablespoon capers, rinsed and drained
2   tablespoons extra-virgin olive oil
4   teaspoons red-wine vinegar
2   teaspoons balsamic vinegar
2   teaspoons fresh thyme, or ¼ teaspoon dried
1   bunch trimmed arugula leaves or watercress sprigs
      (about 2 cups)
    Salt and freshly ground black pepper to taste

1. Cook the beans in boiling water until tender, about 8 minutes; drain and rinse. In a large bowl, combine green beans, tuna, tomatoes, onion and capers. Set aside.

2. In a small bowl, whisk together the olive oil, vinegars and thyme. Add to the tuna mixture along with the arugula or watercress. Toss gently, adding salt and a grinding of black pepper to taste. Serve as a first or main course.

CHICKEN CUTLET SALAD

Makes 4 servings

* *Searing chicken cutlets in a nonstick skillet rather than sautéing them in butter is a good way to brown them outside while keeping them moist and juicy inside.*

* *For a note on Kirby cucumber, see page 52.*

211 CALORIES PER SERVING

20 G PROTEIN

9 G FAT

14 G CARBOHYDRATE

308 MG SODIUM

46 MG CHOLESTEROL

IN THE CHICKEN SALADS OF THE PAST, mayonnaise, with all its concentrated fat and calories, was the dressing of choice. There is life after mayonnaise, however. Salads dressed with a little olive oil, a splash of an acid (in this case, lime juice) and a few fresh herbs or spicy seasonings taste as good or better and are certainly more healthful. This one starts with skinless chicken cutlets—low-fat, quick-cooking and convenient—that have been marinated in crushed garlic, lime juice and jalapeño peppers and quickly seared in a nonstick skillet. The crunchy salsa and generous bed of mixed greens with sprigs of cilantro make this a wholesome, low-fat main-dish salad.

2 tablespoons fresh lime juice

2 garlic cloves, crushed through a press

1 teaspoon olive oil

1 teaspoon seeded, finely chopped jalapeño pepper
   or other fresh chili pepper

Pinch of salt

4 skinless chicken cutlets, pounded thin (about 16 ounces)

Tomato Salsa

2 cups diced (¼-inch) ripe plum tomatoes

½ cup fresh corn kernels, cut from the cob

½ cup diced (¼-inch) seedless cucumber or Kirby cucumber

¼ cup diced (¼-inch) red onion

1 tablespoon extra-virgin olive oil

1 tablespoon fresh lime juice

1 tablespoon finely chopped fresh cilantro or basil

4 cups rinsed, trimmed, torn salad greens
   (red leaf lettuce, romaine and spinach)
¼ cup packed fresh cilantro sprigs
2 teaspoons extra-virgin olive oil
1 teaspoon fresh lime juice
4 lime wedges

1. In a pie plate or deep platter, stir the lime juice, garlic, 1 teaspoon olive oil, chili pepper and salt together. Add the chicken cutlets and turn to coat. Set aside while preparing the salsa or, if preparing ahead, cover and refrigerate until ready to cook.

2. **Just before serving, prepare the salsa:** Combine the tomatoes, corn, cucumber, red onion, 1 tablespoon olive oil, lime juice and cilantro; stir to blend. Set aside.

3. Heat a large (10-to-12-inch) nonstick skillet over medium-high heat until hot enough to evaporate a drop of water upon contact. Add the chicken cutlets and quickly sear until browned on both sides and cooked through, about 2 to 3 minutes per side.

4. Combine the greens and cilantro in a large bowl; add the remaining 2 teaspoons olive oil and 1 teaspoon lime juice; toss to blend. Divide among four large dinner plates. Place a chicken cutlet in the center of each plate and top with a spoonful of the salsa, dividing evenly. Garnish each plate with a lime wedge.

SPINACH, TURKEY & MUSHROOM SALAD

Makes 4 servings

TIPS

✳ *Generally it is possible to lighten a dish by using a small amount of an intensive flavor. Here, the amount of fried bacon has been reduced from four slices to just one finely crumbled slice.*

✳ *Dressings, once based on a formula of three parts oil to one part acid (vinegar or lemon juice), have taken on a new balance in response to concerns about fat. Following a technique that may be applied to many dressings, this one is a sweet-acid mixture made primarily of lime juice, sweetened with a little honey, softened with a minimum of olive oil and spiced with mustard and garlic.*

✳ *For a note on Kirby cucumbers, see page 52.*

A MIXTURE OF SPINACH AND SLICED MUSHROOMS, sprinkled generously with toasted croutons and pieces of bacon and tossed with salad dressing—sometimes made from a portion of the hot bacon fat—has become a luncheon salad special. Because it is strongly flavored, a small amount of the bacon can easily be spread over a large area. In the following recipe, it has been reduced to one crisp, finely crumbled slice for 4 servings.

Dressing

- ¼ cup fresh lime juice
- 1 tablespoon honey
- 2 teaspoons olive oil
- 1 teaspoon whole-grain Dijon-style mustard
- 1 small garlic clove, crushed through a press
  Freshly ground black pepper

Salad

- 1 slice bacon
- 1 tablespoon finely chopped hazelnuts or pecans
- 4 cups washed, trimmed, torn spinach leaves
- 1 cup thinly sliced white button mushrooms
- 1 Kirby cucumber, peeled and thinly sliced
- 1 cup cubed (½-inch) cooked small new (red-skinned) potatoes (about 3)
- 2 ounces thinly sliced smoked turkey, cut into ¼-inch-wide strips

1. **Making the dressing:** In a small bowl, combine the lime juice, honey, olive oil, mustard, garlic and a grinding of black pepper; whisk until blended.

2. **Making the salad:** Cook the bacon; drain on paper towels. Finely chop and set aside. Toast the nuts in a dry skillet over medium-low heat for 1 minute; set aside.

3. Combine the spinach, mushrooms, cucumber, potatoes and turkey in a large bowl. Add the dressing and toss to coat. Sprinkle with the bacon and toasted nuts and serve at once.

144 CALORIES PER SERVING

6 G PROTEIN

6 G FAT

18 G CARBOHYDRATES

91 MG SODIUM

1 MG CHOLESTEROL

ORIENTAL CHICKEN SALAD

Makes 4 servings

293 CALORIES PER SERVING

36 G PROTEIN

13 G FAT

8 G CARBOHYDRATE

293 MG SODIUM

87 MG

MY LEAST FAVORITE RENDITION OF CHICKEN SALAD is the coffee-shop variety that is all white in color and served with an oversized ice-cream scoop. In contrast, this sparkling salad of tender strips of chicken tossed with a rainbow of fresh vegetables is dressed with a tangy mix of tamari (or soy sauce), lemon and lime juice, fresh ginger and sesame oil. Tamari-Garlic Almonds that top the salad are crunchy and delicious, but remember to use nuts judiciously. Although nutritious, they are oily and can add too much fat. When served on a bed of cooled short-grain brown rice, this salad makes enough for 8.

1   chicken (2½-3 pounds) thoroughly rinsed,
      giblets discarded
½   onion
1   bay leaf

Tamari-Garlic Almonds
¼   cup coarsely chopped almonds
2   teaspoons tamari or soy sauce
1   teaspoon vegetable oil
1   teaspoon minced garlic

Salad
3   ounces snow peas, ends trimmed
1   cup thin diagonal slices carrots
¼   cup thin diagonal slices scallions
1   strip (2-x-½-inch) orange zest, cut into julienne strips

Dressing
2   tablespoons fresh lemon juice
1   teaspoon peeled, grated fresh gingerroot

½   teaspoon tamari or soy sauce
½   teaspoon sesame oil
¼   teaspoon hot pepper flakes
1   tablespoon vegetable oil
    Salt and freshly ground black pepper

1. Place the chicken in a large saucepan; cover with water; add the onion and bay leaf. Heat to boiling; cook, uncovered, over low heat, turning the chicken once, until the juices run clear when the bird is pierced with a fork, about 1 hour. Cool in the broth. Remove from the broth; carefully remove and discard the skin. Pull the meat from the bones in large pieces and cut into ½-inch-wide strips; set aside. Discard the bones. (Strain the broth and refrigerate overnight. The next day, skim the solid fat from the top; divide the broth among plastic freezer containers and freeze for another use.)

2. **Making the almonds:** In a small skillet, combine the almonds, tamari or soy sauce, vegetable oil and garlic. Cook, stirring constantly, over low heat, until the nuts are coated and the bottom of the pan is dry, about 3 minutes. Transfer to a plate to cool.

3. **Making the salad:** Heat a small saucepan half-filled with water to boiling; add the snow peas. Cook until they turn bright green, 20 to 30 second. Drain and rinse under cold water; blot dry with a paper towel.

4. In a large bowl, combine the chicken, snow peas, carrots, scallions and orange zest.

5. **Making the dressing:** In a separate bowl, combine the lemon juice, ginger, tamari or soy sauce, sesame oil and hot pepper flakes. Slowly whisk in the vegetable oil until blended.

6. Toss the dressing with the chicken mixture and season to taste with salt and a grinding of black pepper. Sprinkle with the Tamari-Garlic Almonds. Serve at once.

EGG-WHITE EGG SALAD
in TOMATO CUPS

Makes 4 servings

EVEN AS A CHILD, I preferred the white to the yolk of a hard-boiled egg. This pretty egg salad takes the middle ground by using all the whites and only half the yolks in six eggs. Because the salad lacks the warm yellow glow of the extra yolks, I have stuffed it into scooped-out tomato shells to add color. The dressing uses half reduced-fat mayonnaise and half yogurt.

6	hard-boiled eggs
½	cup thinly sliced celery or fennel
½	avocado, peeled, pitted and cut into ¼-inch pieces
3	tablespoons thinly sliced scallions
1	tablespoon pitted, finely chopped brine-cured black olives
2	tablespoons reduced-fat mayonnaise
2	tablespoons low-fat plain yogurt
¼	cup packed fresh basil leaves, torn into small pieces, or fresh Italian (flat-leaf) parsley
2	teaspoons red-wine vinegar
⅛	teaspoon salt
	Freshly ground black pepper to taste
4	large tomatoes
	Small whole basil leaves for garnish

1. Remove 3 of the egg yolks; discard. Cut the remaining eggs and whites into 8 pieces each, approximately ½-inch chunks. Place in a large bowl with the celery or fennel, avocado, scallions and olives.

TIPS

✳ *Eggs are good sources of protein and contain vitamins A, D, B12, calcium, iron and other minerals. The egg yolk contains fat and cholesterol, but the white, a good source of lean protein, has no cholesterol and negligible fat.*

✳ *Reduced-fat mayonnaise contains one-third the fat of regular.*

✳ *To hard-boil eggs, see step 1 on page 60.*

158 CALORIES PER SERVING

9 G PROTEIN

10 G FAT

9 G CARBOHYDRATE

195 MG SODIUM

162 MG CHOLESTEROL

2. In a separate bowl, combine the mayonnaise, yogurt, basil or parsley, vinegar, salt and pepper. Pour over the egg mixture and mix gently.

3. Cut ½ inch from the tops of the tomatoes. Using a teaspoon, scoop out the pulp and seeds, leaving the shell intact. (Discard the pulp and seeds or reserve for another use.) Fill with the egg salad mixture. Garnish the tops with the small whole basil leaves.

GREEN GODDESS DRESSING

Makes about 1⅓ cups

9 CALORIES PER TABLESPOON

I G PROTEIN

0.1 G FAT

I G CARBOHYDRATE

73 MG SODIUM

I MG CHOLESTEROL

DRESSING A SALAD, especially with store-bought bottled dressing, adds fat calories to an otherwise healthful meal. Traditionally, oil and vinegar dressings were made with a ratio of 3 tablespoons of oil to 1 tablespoon of vinegar (or other acid). In the following "creamy" dressing, there is no oil, and a minimum of fat is contributed by the low-fat cottage cheese, anchovy and low-fat milk.

    1   cup low-fat cottage cheese
    ½   cup packed watercress leaves
    ¼   cup skim or low-fat milk
    2   tablespoons chopped fresh dill
    ½   garlic clove, crushed through a press
    ½   teaspoon chopped, rinsed and drained canned anchovy fillet
    ¼   teaspoon salt, or to taste

Place the cottage cheese, watercress, milk, dill, garlic, anchovy and salt in the bowl of a food processor. Process until smooth.

FRESH TOMATO DRESSING

Makes about 1 cup

IN THIS RECIPE, RIPE TOMATOES provide the "acid" in greater quantity than the oil, but with a much sweeter, fruitier result than if lemon juice or vinegar were used. Tossed with herbs and a small amount of olive oil, the tomatoes continue to give off their juice and flavor as they combine with the other ingredients.

1 cup chopped ripe tomatoes with juices
2 teaspoons extra-virgin olive oil
2 teaspoons white-wine vinegar
½ garlic clove, finely chopped or crushed through a press
½ teaspoon fresh thyme leaves, stripped from the stems,
  or pinch dried
¼ teaspoon salt
  Freshly ground black pepper

7 CALORIES PER TABLESPOON

0 G PROTEIN

0.6 G FAT

0 G CARBOHYDRATE

34 MG SODIUM

0 MG CHOLESTEROL

Combine the tomatoes and their juice, olive oil, vinegar, garlic, thyme and salt in a small bowl. Add a grinding of black pepper. Let stand at room temperature until ready to serve.

HONEY-MUSTARD DRESSING

Makes about ¾ cup

ANOTHER NON-OIL DRESSING made with low-fat yogurt balanced with the sweetness of honey and the spice of mustard and vinegar.

½ cup low-fat plain yogurt
4 teaspoons white-wine vinegar
4 teaspoons Dijon-style mustard
1 tablespoon honey
2 tablespoons thinly sliced scallions
¼ teaspoon freshly ground black pepper

13 CALORIES PER TABLESPOON

1 G PROTEIN

0.3 G FAT

2 G CARBOHYDRATE

29 MG SODIUM

1 MG CHOLESTEROL

Combine yogurt, vinegar, mustard, honey, scallions and pepper in a small bowl. Stir with a spoon until thoroughly blended.

Chapter 5

Pizzas, Sandwiches & Burgers

PIZZAS, SANDWICHES & BURGERS

FROM THE BASTIONS OF POWER lunches, where steak sandwiches and jumbo burgers have ruled for decades, to school cafeterias, where ham and cheese on white has been a daily standby for generations, a counterrevolution is in full swing. The business-as-usual slapping of meat and slathering of mayonnaise onto anemic white bread is being challenged on all fronts by ingredients that are fresher, leaner and more exotic than anyone would have imagined a decade ago.

The sandwich, in short, is being reinvented, and the evidence can be found in the lavish use of roasted vegetables, peppery salad greens like watercress and arugula, sprouted clover and garlic, slivered or shredded raw vegetables and the arrival of judicious helpings of flavorful, specialty cheeses and tangy, unconventional mustards.

Where roast beef was once king, the throne is being usurped by grilled chicken breasts, water-packed tuna and intensely smoked turkey.

Pizza, too, is challenging the sandwich as a lunch or light-meal alternative, and its evolution out of predictability has been no less startling. The high-fat all-American standard—pools of oily mozzarella studded with grease-dappled pepperoni—is today countered by lighter, healthier and more interesting new incarnations. Pizza toppings may be as simple as fresh, sliced tomatoes and basil sprinkled with cheese, or thin slices of eggplant brushed with premium olive oil and seasoned with fresh oregano on a thin crust partially made of whole-wheat flour.

Changes like these do much to disprove the impression that grabbing a sandwich or a slice of pizza is a convenient way to avoid nutrition. Actually, the well-constructed sandwich is a model of a good diet: two parts complex carbohydrate (bread) to several parts vitamin-rich vegetables, a smattering of dairy in the form of cheese, sometimes a portion of protein and a very small amount of fat to moisten and flavor the whole.

T O BUILD A SANDWICH that captures the flavor without relying on high-fat foods, begin with sturdy bread: whole-grain, multi-grain, sourdough, crusty peasant-style loaves or thin, pliable pita pockets. Instead of the old lunch-bucket salami and bologna, choose seafood, chicken or turkey. Dressings of vinegar, yogurt and buttermilk work better than mayonnaise from a health perspective. Crunchy relishes add sweetness and juiciness with little or no fat. When I want to use cheeses or meats that tip the fat scale, I take a conservative approach, using a piece not a pile, and fill in the gaps with greens and other vegetables.

The results, ranging from a juicy new chicken hero to a modified classic tuna melt with a decidedly Mediterranean flavor, nudge sandwiches back to where they belong: into the realm of quick, informal, satisfying eating for good health.

Pizza

Sandwiches

Burgers

BASIC PIZZA DOUGH

Makes one 10-inch pizza or four 5-inch individual pizzas

THE FOLLOWING RECIPE FOR PIZZA DOUGH is a standard mixture of flour, water and yeast. Because I like the chewy texture it contributes to the crust, I mix a little whole-wheat flour with the all-purpose flour. An added bonus, of course, is that whole-wheat flour is more nutritious than refined white.

½ cup warm water (105-115 degrees F)
1 teaspoon active dry yeast
½ teaspoon sugar
1 teaspoon olive oil plus more for coating the dough
1 cup plus 1-3 tablespoons all-purpose flour
¼ cup whole-wheat flour
½ teaspoon salt

1. Pour the water into the bowl of a food processor fitted with a metal blade; sprinkle with the yeast and the sugar; process 1 second. Cover and let stand 10 minutes.

2. Add the 1 teaspoon oil, 1 cup of the all-purpose flour, all of the whole-wheat flour and the salt. Process until blended, about 10 seconds. Add enough of the remaining all-purpose flour, 1 tablespoon at a time, processing 1 second after each addition, until the dough is soft but not sticky.

3. Remove the metal blade and turn the dough out onto a work surface lightly dusted with flour. Knead until the dough springs back when gently poked with a fingertip, about 3 minutes. Shape into a smooth ball.

4. Brush a bowl with a thin coating of olive oil. Add the dough; turn to coat. Cover with plastic wrap and let rise in a warm spot until doubled in bulk, 1 to 1½ hours. Use immediately or freeze.

TIPS

❋ *Making individual pizzas is an excellent way to control portion size.*

❋ *To make dough one day ahead, mix and knead as directed; place in a bowl, cover and refrigerate overnight. Remove from the refrigerator and let rise in a warm place.*

❋ *To freeze dough, mix, knead and let rise, then place in a heavy-duty, tightly closed plastic bag.*

❋ *To make dough without a food processor, mix in a large bowl as directed, but stir in 1 cup of the all-purpose flour by hand until the dough is soft but not sticky. Then knead in the remaining flour until the dough is smooth, 8 to 10 minutes.*

163 CALORIES PER SERVING

5 G PROTEIN

2 G FAT

32 G CARBOHYDRATE

269 MG SODIUM

0 MG CHOLESTEROL

133

SAUSAGE & THREE PEPPER PIZZA

Makes 4 servings

TIPS

✳ *Try these pizza variations:*

■ *Thin sliced tomato, fresh basil leaves and shredded mozzarella*

■ *Oven-Roasted Eggplant (page 142), roasted peppers and grated Parmesan*

■ *Sautéed spinach, sautéed mushrooms, thyme and shredded mozzarella.*

✳ *A sweet red bell pepper is actually a mature green bell pepper; yellow bell peppers are another variety. All three are good sources of vitamin C, and the red and yellow varieties are especially high in vitamin A.*

✳ *If you want to cut fat and calories even further, look for flavorful Italian-style turkey sausage links, available in most supermarkets.*

THIS PIZZA IS A PERFECT EXAMPLE of how to use less of a high-fat ingredient—in this case, Italian sausage—and fill in for any missing flavor with a variety of tasty vegetables. Using vegetables to top pizza is not a newfangled notion: the Italians long ago made it a tradition.

> Basic Pizza Dough (page 133)
> 2 links (about 2 ounces) sweet or hot Italian sausage, removed from casings, or Italian-style turkey sausage
> ½ *each* red, green and yellow bell pepper, seeds, stems and ribs removed, cut into thin lengthwise slices
> 1 teaspoon olive oil plus more to oil pan
> 1 garlic clove, crushed through a press
> 1 teaspoon minced fresh oregano leaves, or ¼ teaspoon dried
> Coarsely ground black pepper
> 1 tablespoon grated Parmesan cheese, preferably Parmigiano-Reggiano

1. Make Basic Pizza Dough.

2. Crumble the sausage into a medium (8-to-10-inch) nonstick skillet and cook, stirring, until browned; transfer to a strainer to drain off the fat. Wipe out the skillet with a paper towel.

3. Add the pepper strips and the oil; toss to blend. Cover and cook over medium-low heat until almost tender, about 5 minutes. Uncover and cook, stirring, over high heat for 2 minutes. Stir in the garlic and oregano and cook for 1 minute. Season with black pepper and let stand off the heat.

4. Preheat the oven to 425 degrees F. Punch down the dough, cover with a cloth and let rest 5 minutes. Brush a 10- or 12-inch pizza pan or a loose-bottomed tart pan lightly with oil. Roll the dough to fit the pan. Transfer to the pan, cover with a towel and let stand 10 minutes.

5. Spoon the pepper mixture evenly over the dough. Sprinkle with the reserved sausage. Sprinkle with the grated cheese.

6. Bake directly on the bottom of the oven or on the lowest oven rack until the edges are browned, 12 to 15 minutes. To serve, cut into wedges.

222 CALORIES PER SERVING

8 G PROTEIN

6 G FAT

34 G CARBOHYDRATE

298 MG SODIUM

1 MG CHOLESTEROL

BROCCOLI, RED ONION & GARLIC PIZZA

Makes 4 servings

THIS SIMPLE, FRESH-TASTING PIZZA illustrates what the topping for the dish was originally meant to be: bright vegetables and just a sprinkling of delicious cheese. Garlic browned in a small amount of olive oil and tossed with broccoli adds flavor with just a little fat.

Basic Pizza Dough (page 133)

2 cups coarsely chopped (about ¼-to-½-inch pieces) broccoli

2 teaspoons olive oil

1 garlic clove, finely chopped

½ cup red onion rings cut from a small onion

1 tablespoon torn fresh basil leaves or fresh Italian (flat-leaf) parsley

3 tablespoons crumbled fresh goat cheese (half a 3.5-ounce log)

1. Make Basic Pizza Dough.

2. Steam the broccoli in a vegetable steamer set over 1 inch of gently boiling water. Cover and cook until crisp-tender, about 3 minutes. Cool and blot dry on paper towels.

3. Combine the oil and garlic in a small skillet; heat over low heat, stirring, just until the garlic begins to sizzle. Remove the skillet from the heat. Add the broccoli and toss to coat.

4. Preheat oven to 425 degrees F. Punch down the dough; cover with a cloth and let rest 10 minutes. Brush a 10- or 12-inch pizza pan or loose-bottomed tart pan lightly with oil. Roll the dough to fit the pan. Transfer to the pan; cover with a towel and let stand 10 minutes.

5. Spoon the broccoli mixture evenly over the prepared dough. Add the onion rings and the basil or parsley; sprinkle with the goat cheese.

6. Bake directly on the bottom of the oven or on the lowest oven rack until the edges are browned, 12 to 15 minutes.

7. To serve, cut into wedges.

NIÇOISE-STYLE PIZZA

Makes 4 servings

270 CALORIES PER SERVING

17 G PROTEIN

6 G FAT

36 G CARBOHYDRATE

471 MG SODIUM

18 MG CHOLESTEROL

A HEARTY TOPPING OF TUNA AND GREEN BEANS makes this a satisfying main dish. Fresh tomatoes and sun-dried tomatoes add flavor and nutrients—without fat. Black olives, although delicious, are used sparingly because they are rich in oil.

Basic Pizza Dough (page 133)

2 ounces fresh green beans, trimmed and cut into 1-inch lengths

3 teaspoons olive oil plus a little more for brushing on dough

½ teaspoon minced fresh rosemary, or pinch dried

1 can (6 ounces) water-packed tuna, drained and blotted dry with a paper towel

1 tablespoon finely chopped sun-dried tomato

1 tablespoon finely chopped onion

1 garlic clove, crushed through a press

1 teaspoon rinsed, drained capers
Freshly ground black pepper

3 cherry tomatoes, cut into thin, round slices

1 tablespoon coarsely chopped fresh Italian (flat-leaf) parsley leaves

2 brine-cured black olives (Kalamata), pitted and coarsely chopped

1. Make Basic Pizza Dough.

2. Blanch the green beans in boiling water until tender, about 3 minutes. Drain, rinse with cold water and blot dry with paper towels. Toss with 1 teaspoon of the olive oil and the rosemary; set aside.

3. In a bowl, combine the tuna, the remaining 2 teaspoons olive oil, sun-dried tomato, onion, garlic, capers and a grinding of black pepper; stir to blend.

4. Preheat oven to 425 degrees F. Punch down the dough; cover with a cloth and let rest 10 minutes. Brush a 10- or 12-inch pizza pan or loose-bottomed tart pan lightly with olive oil. Roll the dough into a circle large enough to fit the pan. Carefully transfer the dough to the pan, pressing it against the rim of the pan. Cover with a towel and let stand 10 minutes.

5. Spoon the tuna mixture evenly over the surface of the dough. Arrange the tomato slices evenly on top of the tuna; add the parsley. Sprinkle evenly with the green bean mixture and top with the black olives.

6. Bake directly on the bottom of the oven or on the lowest oven rack until the edges are well browned, 12 to 15 minutes.

THE NEW HERO

Makes 1 serving

561 CALORIES PER SERVING

30 G PROTEIN

12 G FAT

80 G CARBOHYDRATE

980 MG SODIUM

43 MG CHOLESTEROL

ALTHOUGH THE HERO IS A POPULAR TRADITION in the sandwich culture of America, I have never understood the allure of eating half a pound of cold cuts and cheese. This hero comes to the rescue, not only nutritionally but aesthetically as well.

Oven-Roasted Eggplant slices (page 142)
Vegetable-oil cooking spray
1   chicken cutlet (about 3 ounces), pounded thin

DRESSING
1   teaspoon olive oil
1   teaspoon red-wine vinegar
¼   teaspoon minced fresh oregano leaves, or pinch dried
⅛   teaspoon minced garlic
    Pinch of salt
    Coarsely ground black pepper
1   roasted red bell pepper (either fresh-roasted and seeded
      and peeled or the jarred variety, rinsed and patted dry)

1   Italian hero roll or 6-inch piece of Italian bread,
      halved lengthwise
4-5   arugula leaves or watercress sprigs
2   tablespoons shredded low-fat mozzarella cheese

1. Prepare the eggplant.

2. Heat a medium (8-to-10-inch) nonstick skillet over medium heat until hot enough to evaporate a drop of water upon contact. Spray with vegetable-oil cooking spray. Add the chicken cutlet and cook, turning, until browned on both sides

and no longer pink in the center, about 2 to 3 minutes per side.

3. **Meanwhile, make the dressing:** Combine the oil, vinegar, oregano, garlic, salt and pepper in a shallow bowl. Add the roasted pepper and turn to coat evenly.

4. Open the bread and pull out some of the soft insides. Arrange the arugula leaves or watercress sprigs on both sides of the bread. Place 3 slices of eggplant on one side of the bread. Lift the roasted pepper from the dressing and arrange on top of the eggplant. Top with the mozzarella. Drizzle any remaining dressing over the chicken cutlet and place on the other side of the bread. Fold up the sandwich and halve before serving.

TIP

✳ *Any leftover slices can be served as a vegetable side dish. Or cut them into cubes and toss them with chopped fresh tomato and basil and serve over cooked pasta.*

46 CALORIES PER SERVING

I G PROTEIN

2 G FAT

6 G CARBOHYDRATE

3 MG SODIUM

O MG CHOLESTEROL

OVEN-ROASTED EGGPLANT

Makes 4 servings

TRADITIONALLY, EGGPLANT IS FRIED IN OLIVE OIL. The physiology of this vegetable is similar to a sponge, with the result that eggplant that has been fried is often very oily. In this oven-roasted method, the amount of oil is controlled by lightly brushing each slice with a specific amount.

1   medium-sized eggplant, trimmed and peeled
2   teaspoons olive oil
½   garlic clove, crushed through a press

1. Preheat oven to 425 degrees F. Cut the eggplant into ¼-inch-thick rounds; arrange in a single layer on a nonstick baking sheet. Stir the oil and garlic together in a small bowl and lightly brush on both sides of the eggplant.

2. Roast the eggplant until lightly browned, turning once, about 25 minutes. Use for The New Hero (page 140) or as a topping for Sausage & Three Pepper Pizza (page 134).

GRILLED CHEESE PITA POCKETS

Makes 1 serving

THIS ADAPTATION OF THE GRILLED CHEESE SANDWICH stretches reduced-fat mozzarella, Cheddar or Jarlsberg with sliced tomatoes, bell peppers, dill pickles and alfalfa sprouts. Tucking all these ingredients into a pita pocket keeps them snug between the bread and prevents them from spilling out over the pan. A nonstick skillet is essential for this sandwich.

* *The fillings can vary, but when stuffing the sandwich, make sure to keep the cheese next to the bread so it can melt easily; stuff the vegetables and other fillings into the center.*

206 CALORIES PER SERVING

13 G PROTEIN

7 G FAT

25 G CARBOHYDRATE

501 MG SODIUM

19 MG CHOLESTEROL

- 1 whole-wheat or plain pita
- 1 ounce sliced, reduced-fat cheese (Jarlsberg, Monterey Jack, Cheddar or mozzarella)
- 3 paper-thin slices tomato
- ⅓ cup alfalfa sprouts
- 4 paper-thin slices dill pickle
- 3 paper-thin rings red, green or yellow bell pepper, seeds, stem and ribs removed

  Vegetable-oil cooking spray

1. Cut a thin strip from one side of the pita. Carefully open the pita to make a pocket for the filling.

2. Place one slice of cheese in the pita pocket. Slide in the tomatoes, add the alfalfa sprouts and top with the pickle slices and pepper rings. Then add the remaining cheese slice.

3. Heat a medium (8-to-10-inch) skillet over medium-high heat until hot enough to evaporate a drop of water upon contact. Spray with a coating of vegetable-oil cooking spray. Place the sandwich in the skillet and cook, covered, over medium-low heat, turning once, until browned on both sides, about 10 minutes.

VEGETARIAN SALAD PITAS
with SPICY CHICK-PEA
DRESSING

Makes 4 servings

175 CALORIES PER SERVING

7 G PROTEIN

4 G FAT

286 G CARBOHYDRATE

301 MG SODIUM

0 MG CHOLESTEROL

THIS IS A TAKEOFF ON A FALAFEL SANDWICH, a deep-fried chick-pea patty topped with lettuce, tomato and tahini sauce and stuffed into a pita. Here, the order is reversed: the vegetables have become the filling, and the chick-peas provide the sauce.

1	cup coarsely chopped (¼-inch pieces) broccoli florets
½	cup thinly sliced carrots
½	cup fresh or frozen peas
¼	cup chopped, peeled broccoli stems
¼	cup chopped red bell pepper
¼	cup chopped fresh Italian (flat-leaf) parsley
1	tablespoon chopped fresh dill
4	pita breads
	Spicy Chick-Pea Dressing (opposite page)

1. Place the broccoli florets, carrots, peas and broccoli stems in a steamer rack set over 1 inch of boiling water. Cover and cook 4 minutes; rinse to cool. Drain on a double thickness of paper towel.

2. Combine the steamed vegetables with the red pepper, parsley and dill. Slit the tops of the pitas and fill with the vegetables. Top each with a spoonful of Spicy Chick-Pea Dressing.

SPICY CHICK-PEA DRESSING

Makes about ⅔ cup

THIS ZESTY PUREE OF CHICK-PEAS, garlic and cottage cheese is smooth and creamy. It is also delicious served as a dressing over salad greens.

½ cup cooked dried or rinsed canned chick-peas
1 tablespoon coarsely chopped garlic
3 tablespoons water
3 tablespoons fresh lemon juice
2 tablespoons olive oil
2 tablespoons low-fat cottage cheese
Tabasco or other hot sauce to taste
Salt to taste

37 CALORIES PER TABLESPOON
I G PROTEIN
3 G FAT
2 G CARBOHYDRATE
48 MG SODIUM
O MG CHOLESTEROL

Place the chick-peas, garlic, water, lemon juice, olive oil and cottage cheese in the bowl of a food processor or blender. Blend until smooth. Add the Tabasco and salt to taste. Serve on Vegetarian Salad Pitas (opposite page).

SALMON SALAD SANDWICHES

Makes 4 servings

ALTHOUGH NOT AS POPULAR AS CANNED TUNA, salmon makes a delicious sandwich. A small amount of olive oil is used to moisten the salmon and form a spreadable paste. Serve on a small roll or spread on thick slices of white or multi-grain bread. The avocado lends richness, while the chopped apple adds crunch and sweet flavor.

1	can (7½ ounces) red or pink salmon, or 1 cup cooked, skinned and boned salmon, flaked
⅓	cup chopped unpeeled Granny Smith apple
¼	cup chopped seedless cucumber
¼	cup chopped red onion
1	tablespoon chopped fresh basil or fresh Italian (flat-leaf) parsley
1	tablespoon fresh lime juice
1	tablespoon olive oil
½	teaspoon peeled, grated fresh gingerroot
8	slices extra-thin white or multi-grain bread
½	cup peeled, pitted and mashed ripe avocado

1. Combine the salmon, apple, cucumber, onion and basil or parsley. Set aside.

2. Stir together the lime juice, olive oil and ginger. Add to the salmon mixture and stir to blend.

3. Spread each slice of bread with 1 tablespoon of the mashed avocado. Spread the salmon mixture evenly on 4 slices of the bread. Top with the remaining slices of bread. Trim the crusts and cut each sandwich into 4 triangles.

ITALIAN-STYLE TUNA MELT

Makes 2 servings

THE TRADITIONAL TUNA MELT is usually a bland, white mixture bound with mayonnaise, open-faced, covered with slices of melted Cheddar-style cheese. This colorful, zesty version relies on red-wine vinegar and other Italian ingredients instead of mayonnaise and is topped with slices of fresh tomatoes.

1   can (6½ ounces) Italian-style tuna in olive oil, well drained
¼   cup chopped red onion
¼   cup chopped celery
1   tablespoon chopped fresh Italian (flat-leaf) parsley
1   tablespoon red-wine vinegar
1   teaspoon rinsed, drained small capers
2   large slices (about ½-inch-thick) peasant-style Italian bread
½   garlic clove
2   teaspoons extra-virgin olive oil
4   thin slices tomato
2   thin slices (about 2 ounces) skim-milk mozzarella

405 CALORIES PER SERVING

37 G PROTEIN

16 G FAT

26 G CARBOHYDRATE

670 MG SODIUM

32 MG CHOLESTEROL

1. Combine the tuna, red onion, celery, parsley, vinegar and capers. Set aside.

2. Heat the broiler. Rub the bread lightly with the cut side of the garlic. Brush both sides with 1 teaspoon olive oil. Place on a baking sheet and toast, about 3 inches from the heat source, until golden, about 3 to 5 minutes, depending on the heat of the broiler. Turn the bread over and toast the other side. Remove from the broiler.

3. Arrange the tomato slices on the toast. Mound the tuna mixture on top and top each with a slice of mozzarella. Broil until the cheese melts, about 3 minutes. Serve warm.

GROUND TURKEY BURGER
with CRUNCHY CELERY RELISH

Makes 4 servings

TIRED OF FATTY HAMBURGERS? Bored with bland ground turkey? Try this version of ground turkey filled with a small portion of blue cheese, zapped with Tabasco sauce and garnished with crunchy relish.

1¼   pounds ground turkey
¼   cup (about 1 ounce) crumbled blue cheese

Celery Relish
2   cups long, thin, diagonal slices celery
½   cup thinly sliced red onion
2   tablespoons cider vinegar
1   teaspoon sugar
    Tabasco sauce to taste

4   slices whole-wheat toast or pita pockets

1. Divide the turkey into 8 even patties. Place 1 tablespoon of the blue cheese in the center of 4 of them, top with the other 4 patties and seal them together.

2. Heat a large nonstick skillet over medium-high heat until hot enough to evaporate a drop of water upon contact. Add the burgers and cook over high heat until seared, about 3 minutes. Turn the burgers, reduce heat to medium, cover and cook until cooked through, 8 to 10 minutes.

3. **Meanwhile, make the relish:** Stir together the celery, onion, vinegar and sugar. Set aside.

4. Uncover the burgers and sprinkle with the Tabasco to taste; turn and sprinkle the other side with Tabasco. Remove from the skillet and serve, topped with a portion of the celery relish, open-faced on toast or tucked into a warmed pita.

Chapter 6

VEGETABLES,
GRAINS, BEANS
& POTATOES

VEGETABLES, GRAINS, BEANS & POTATOES

JUST BEFORE I WAS MARRIED, I discovered that my future husband thought all vegetables came from a can. His idea of excitement was a pile of pale green peas served with a lump of melted butter. I had never eaten a canned pea. Growing up, I had been accustomed to vegetables being as important as the entrée. At home, my mother baked artichokes, mushrooms and zucchini and boiled fresh dandelion greens, mustard greens, broccoli rabe, escarole, cauliflower and spinach—serving them all with olive oil and garlic. Mother's vegetables were definitely a main event.

During the years we've been married, my husband has gradually been converted to fresh vegetables, and they are no longer relegated to the side of his plate. In the rest of the country, too, people have been eating their vegetables. In 1965, the average produce department carried only 65 items; by 1980, it had swelled to 250. As a result, a new vegetable heritage has emerged, with Asian and tropical varieties that would have once been unimaginable served regularly throughout North America.

At the stove, the two-quart saucepan no longer reigns supreme but has been joined by a battery of new equipment. Collapsible vegetable steamers are now standard. My mother cooks her broccoli in the microwave and has made room in her cabinet for a nonstick skillet so she can use less oil when she stir-fries.

Instead of boiling vegetables, I've happened upon an equally efficient method that gives them more concentrated flavor: oven-roasting. Drizzled with a little olive oil and roasted in a moderate or hot oven, vegetables emerge nicely soft or appropriately crunchy, never waterlogged. Root vegetables—beets, carrots, sweet potatoes, onions and garlic—whose natural sugars caramelize in the oven, take exceptionally well to roasting, but asparagus and green and red peppers also benefit from it.

PROVIDED THAT TOO MUCH OIL is not added in the process, stir-frying can transform vegetables from an afterthought to a main feature, one that can incorporate any number of choices, as the produce counter or the garden dictates. My own version, finished off with some crunchy soy almonds, needs only a mound of rice to be called dinner.

The rice, however, may not necessarily be white. In fact, it is usually the more nutritious brown or aromatic basmati, now increasingly common in supermarkets. I am just as likely to serve quick grains and beans like orzo, barley or lentils. In place of the once obligatory square of butter (or in the case of baked beans, pork fat), I toss in raisins, nuts, spices, orange or lemon zest, ginger, garlic, chili peppers, smoky-tasting cilantro or lean ham.

Even in mashed potatoes, I refuse to accept old-fashioned quantities of fat: yogurt replaces cream or whole milk, and a tiny pool of butter melted on top of each serving makes up the difference.

BRAISED GREENS

Makes 4 servings

THIS IS A SIMPLE, FAST AND NUTRITIOUS WAY to prepare endive, chicory, tender beet tops, spinach, kale, collards, Swiss chard, Chinese cabbage or the dark green outside leaves of romaine lettuce.

102 CALORIES PER SERVING

21 G PROTEIN

4 G FAT

17 G CARBOHYDRATE

42 MG SODIUM

0 MG CHOLESTEROL

2   pounds greens, washed, woody stalks trimmed, torn into
      2-inch pieces

1   tablespoon extra-virgin olive oil

1   garlic clove, crushed through a press

1   tablespoon red-wine vinegar

1. Boil the greens in plenty of boiling salted water until tender, 5 to 10 minutes, depending on the type of green. Drain well.

2. Combine the oil and garlic in a large (10-to-12-inch) skillet; stir over low heat just until the garlic begins to sizzle. Add the greens all at once and stir just to coat. Splash with the vinegar; stir again. Serve at once.

STIR-FRIED VEGETABLES
with SOY ALMONDS

Makes 4 to 6 servings

TIP

✳ *Steaming crunchy vegetables such as carrots and broccoli shortens the cooking time and avoids the temptation to add more oil.*

70 CALORIES PER SERVING

2 G PROTEIN

3 G FAT

10 G CARBOHYDRATE

165 MG SODIUM

0 MG CHOLESTEROL

FUELED BY OUR CONTINUED INTEREST in Asian cuisines, the stir-fry is becoming a North American classic. It is quick and easy, uses a minimum of fat and, when served over rice, is a satisfying meatless main dish. A heavy-handed cook, however, can transform it into an oily, high-fat one. To stir-fry vegetables with a minimum of fat, start with 2 teaspoons vegetable oil to heat the garlic and ginger quickly, then add the vegetables. A little chicken broth in place of oil helps keep the vegetables moist while cooking. During the last 30 seconds, add a drop of toasted sesame oil and a drizzle of soy sauce. Any combination of raw or cooked vegetables can be used. Serve as a side dish or over rice as a main dish. The soy almonds are a treat for when you feel like splurging.

1-2	cups broccoli florets
1	cup diagonal slices (¼-inch) carrot
2	teaspoons vegetable oil
1	teaspoon finely chopped garlic
1	teaspoon peeled, finely chopped fresh gingerroot
1-2	cups trimmed, chopped (1-inch) green beans, asparagus or snow peas
1	cup slivered (¼-x-1-inch) red, green and/or yellow bell pepper
2-3	teaspoons reduced-sodium or homemade chicken broth (page 75), or as needed
1-2	tablespoons reduced-sodium soy sauce
½	teaspoon sesame oil
1-2	scallions, trimmed and cut into thin diagonal slices
	Soy Almonds (opposite page)

1. Steam the broccoli and carrots in a covered vegetable steamer over an inch of boiling water for 3 minutes.

2. Heat a large (10-to-12-inch) nonstick skillet over medium-high heat until hot enough to evaporate a drop of water upon contact. Add the oil, garlic and ginger; stir-fry 10 seconds.

3. Gradually add all the vegetables except the scallions, stirring constantly over high heat. Sprinkle with the chicken broth. Stir-fry until the vegetables are crisp-tender, 3 to 5 minutes.

4. Stir in the soy sauce and sesame oil. Remove from the heat. Spoon into a serving bowl and top with the scallions and the Soy Almonds, if using.

SOY ALMONDS

Makes about ¼ cup

ALTHOUGH ALMONDS ARE TOUTED AS BEING NUTRITIOUS, all nuts are oily and therefore high in fat and calories. This recipe offers a good example of how to use a high-fat, highly flavored ingredient sparingly in order to get the full benefits of its taste.

¼ cup whole natural (unblanched) almonds
½ teaspoon vegetable oil
1 tablespoon reduced-sodium soy sauce

Combine the almonds and oil in a large (10-inch) skillet; heat, stirring, over medium-high heat, until toasted, about 3 minutes. Add the soy sauce and cook, stirring, until the soy sauce boils and coats the almonds, about 2 minutes. Transfer to a paper towel to blot dry. Coarsely chop and serve on Stir-Fried Vegetables (opposite page).

TIP

* *Chop Soy Almonds finely and sprinkle over steamed broccoli or salads.*

50 CALORIES PER TABLESPOON
2 G PROTEIN
4 G FAT
2 G CARBOHYDRATE
133 MG SODIUM
0 MG CHOLESTEROL.

SMOTHERED SPINACH

Makes 4 servings

51 CALORIES PER SERVING

5 G PROTEIN

2 G FAT

7 G CARBOHYDRATE

122 MG SODIUM

0 MG CHOLESTEROL

I NEVER LIKED CREAMED SPINACH MUCH, though I do love this vegetable in a fresher preparation. When the whole leaves are steamed gently on a collapsible steamer, they emerge bright green, tender and intact after just a few minutes over boiling water. They can then be "stir-fried" with a dash of olive oil, a smidgen of garlic and some lemon juice.

2 pounds fresh spinach leaves, thoroughly rinsed,
   stems trimmed
1 teaspoon extra-virgin olive oil
1 small garlic clove, crushed through a press
1 teaspoon fresh lemon juice

1. Pour 1 inch of water into a large (6-to-8-quart) saucepan; place a folding steaming rack in the saucepan; heat the water to boiling.

2. Add the spinach; cover and steam just until the spinach wilts, 3 to 5 minutes.

3. Protecting your hand with a mitt, lift the steaming rack from the saucepan. Discard the water (or reserve for vegetable broth) and wipe the pan dry.

4. Add the oil and the garlic to the pan; cook, stirring, over low heat until the garlic begins to sizzle, about 30 seconds. Stir in the cooked spinach just to coat lightly with the oil.

5. Sprinkle with the lemon juice and serve immediately.

ROASTED LEEKS

Makes 4 servings

LEEKS ARE MISUNDERSTOOD BY THE AVERAGE COOK. Many people expect these members of the onion family to have a strong oniony flavor. In fact, leeks—especially cooked leeks—have a mild sweet taste and a silky texture. More than an obscure ingredient in a soup pot, they make a delectable side dish or salad course. They are low in calories and a good source of fiber.

2 leeks (about 8 ounces each), trimmed, split lengthwise
    and washed thoroughly
¼ cup reduced-sodium or homemade chicken broth (page 75)
1 tablespoon grated Parmesan cheese, preferably
    Parmigiano-Reggiano
    Freshly ground black pepper

1. Preheat oven to 350 degrees F. Arrange the trimmed leeks in a 13-x-9-inch baking dish; add the broth.

2. Cover with foil and bake for about 25 minutes, or until the leeks are fork-tender. Uncover and sprinkle evenly with the grated cheese and a grinding of black pepper.

3. Bake, uncovered, until the cheese melts and turns golden, about 5 minutes.

TIPS

❋ *The melting properties of imported Parmigiano-Reggiano cheese are superior to other types of Parmesan. However, it should be used with a light hand. The taste is concentrated, but because it is a low-moisture, aged, dry cheese, the fat, too, is concentrated.*

❋ *Leeks can be very sandy. For easy washing, I usually split them lengthwise and coax the sand out from between the many layers by soaking them first in warm water and then in cold.*

❋ *Make sure that the leeks are fresh, not woody or dry.*

28 CALORIES PER SERVING

I G PROTEIN

I G FAT

5 G CARBOHYDRATE

39 MG SODIUM

I MG CHOLESTEROL

ROASTED ONIONS

Makes 4 servings

A FRESH-TASTING, DELICIOUS SUBSTITUTE for the traditional creamed onions that my mother made every Thanksgiving—and usually forgot to serve. As these large Spanish onions slowly bake, their natural sugars caramelize and they become silken and sweet. Then crumbs are added and browned for the last 10 minutes. The taste is unforgettable.

2 large sweet Spanish onions (about 8 ounces each),
     peeled and trimmed
2 teaspoons olive oil, preferably extra-virgin
   Salt
   Freshly ground black pepper
1 fresh sage leaf, torn into 4 pieces, or ¼ teaspoon dried

Crumbs
¾ cup coarse bread crumbs made from day-old Italian bread
2 teaspoons olive oil, preferably extra-virgin
1 small garlic clove, crushed through a press
½ teaspoon minced fresh sage leaves, or ¼ teaspoon dried

1. Preheat oven to 350 degrees F. Cut the onions in half crosswise and trim the pointed ends so the onions will sit evenly. Arrange them in a square baking dish just large enough to hold them comfortably (a 9-inch square pan is good) so that their widest part faces up.

2. Top each onion with ½ teaspoon olive oil, a few grains of salt, a sprinkling of black pepper and a piece of fresh sage leaf or a pinch of dried. Cover the baking dish tightly with aluminum foil and bake until the onions are very tender and a pale straw color, about 50 minutes.

3. **Meanwhile, prepare the crumbs:** In a bowl, combine the crumbs, 2 teaspoons olive oil, the garlic and the minced sage leaves or ¼ teaspoon dried; toss with a fork until blended.

4. Remove the foil from the baking dish. Carefully spoon the crumbs onto the surface of each onion and press them down. Bake, uncovered, until golden, about 15 minutes. Serve warm or at room temperature.

ROASTED SWEET POTATOES

Makes 4 to 6 servings

217 CALORIES PER SERVING

3 G PROTEIN

O G FAT

52 G CARBOHYDRATE

86 MG SODIUM

O MG CHOLESTEROL

ONE OF THE BEST EXAMPLES of the American sweet tooth is our collective fondness for sweet potatoes baked with brown sugar, raisins and melted marshmallows. In fact, this vegetable, whose natural sweetness is unequaled by any other, needs little added sugar. In this recipe, apple juice glazes the sweet potatoes, adding a slightly acid flavor to balance the "sweets."

2 pounds sweet potatoes, peeled and cut crosswise
   into ¾-inch-thick rounds
¾ cup unsweetened apple juice
2 tablespoons dried currants
¼ teaspoon ground or crushed whole allspice
   Pinch of salt

1. Preheat oven to 350 degrees F. Arrange the sweet potato slices in a single layer in a large roasting pan. Add the apple juice, currants and allspice.

2. Cover with aluminum foil and bake until the potatoes are fork-tender, about 30 minutes. Uncover and turn the potatoes. Bake, uncovered, turning once halfway through baking, until the apple juice cooks down and thickens and the potatoes turn golden, about 20 minutes.

3. Sprinkle with a little salt.

ROASTED CARROTS
with GARLIC

Makes 4 servings

OVEN-ROASTING CARAMELIZES THE NATURAL SUGARS, while the dry heat intensifies the taste. Carrots are an excellent source of vitamin A.

4 large carrots (about 1 pound), peeled, trimmed
     and split lengthwise
1 tablespoon olive oil, preferably extra-virgin
2 tablespoons water
8 small garlic cloves, peeled but left whole
    Pinch of salt
    Freshly ground black pepper

78 CALORIES PER SERVING

1 G PROTEIN

4 G FAT

11 G CARBOHYDRATE

135 MG SODIUM

0 MG CHOLESTEROL

1. Preheat oven to 350 degrees F. Arrange the carrots in a 13-x-9-inch baking dish. Add the oil, water and garlic. Cover with foil and bake until the carrots are fork-tender, about 30 minutes.

2. Uncover and turn the carrots. Bake until they are golden, about 10 minutes. Sprinkle with the salt and pepper.

ROASTED BEETS
with ORANGE

Makes 4 servings

TIP

✳ *This method also works with onions, carrots, potatoes and other root vegetables.*

44 CALORIES PER SERVING

I G PROTEIN

2 G FAT

5 G CARBOHYDRATE

104 MG SODIUM

0 MG CHOLESTEROL

T RADITIONALLY, BEETS ARE BOILED IN WATER, robbing them of much of their flavor and texture. The following technique of wrapping them individually in foil and oven-roasting them intensifies their sweetness, giving them an almost silken texture. Depending on their size, roasted beets take at least an hour to bake. Serve them warm as a vegetable or cold as a salad.

4   large (about 2 inches in diameter) beets, washed,
      tops trimmed
2   teaspoons extra-virgin olive oil
4   fresh basil or sage leaves or ½-inch leafy sprig fresh thyme,
      or pinch dried sage or thyme
2   strips (½-x-2-inch) orange zest, cut into julienne strips
    1 garlic clove, finely chopped
    Pinch of salt

1. Preheat oven to 350 degrees F. Using a vegetable peeler, remove the outside layer of the beets. Trim the tops and bottoms so they are flat. Cut 4 pieces of aluminum foil large enough to wrap each beet. Place a beet in the center of each piece of foil.

2. Top each beet with ½ teaspoon olive oil. Place the fresh or dried herbs, a strip or two of orange zest, a pinch of garlic and salt on top of each beet. Wrap tightly in foil and place directly on the oven rack. Bake until tender when pierced with a skewer, 1 to 1½ hours. Let stand until cool enough to handle. Carefully peel off the foil. Cut the beets into slices and serve with any juices left in the foil.

ROASTED ASPARAGUS

Makes 4 servings

THE FLAVOR OF ASPARAGUS that has been oven-roasted is more intense than asparagus that has been steamed. Oven-roasting concentrates the flavors, rather than diluting them. The oils in the strips of lemon zest (the yellow part of the rind) perfume the asparagus.

1 bunch asparagus, moderately thin, rinsed and trimmed
1 tablespoon olive oil, preferably extra-virgin
3 strips (2-x-½-inch) lemon zest, removed with a vegetable
   peeler, cut into long, thin (¹⁄₁₆-inch) strips
1 teaspoon fresh thyme leaves, stripped from the stems,
   or pinch dried
   Freshly ground black pepper
   Fresh thyme sprigs for garnish

1. Preheat oven to 425 degrees F. Arrange the asparagus in a 13-x-9-inch baking pan. Drizzle with the olive oil, scatter over the lemon zest and sprinkle with the thyme. Toss to coat.

2. Roast the asparagus for 10 minutes; stir. Roast until the asparagus is tender, about 2 to 5 minutes more. Sprinkle with black pepper and garnish with thyme sprigs.

✳ To keep fresh thyme or other fresh herbs for up to 2 weeks, stand the herb sprigs in a glass with a little water covering the stems, place a plastic bag over the glass and store in the refrigerator. Change the water every couple of days.

✳ For this recipe, it's especially important to buy asparagus that is fresh, not old or woody.

57 CALORIES PER SERVING

3 G PROTEIN;

4 G FAT

5 G CARBOHYDRATE

4 MG SODIUM

0 MG CHOLESTEROL

BARLEY & BROWN RICE PILAF

Makes 6 servings

225 CALORIES PER SERVING

6 G PROTEIN

5 G FAT

39 G CARBOHYDRATE

27 MG SODIUM

0 MG CHOLESTEROL

BARLEY, LOW IN FAT BUT HIGH IN FIBER and a good source of vegetable protein, is a much-neglected grain in the North American diet. Fully 90 percent of it goes to livestock for feed and to breweries for beer. Although many people seem to suffer from fear of barley, the truth is, cooking it is as easy—or easier—than cooking pasta. Inexpensive, it is available in most supermarkets. "Pearl" barley indicates that the tough outer hull has been removed; when a package is labeled simply "barley" and the grain looks creamy-white, it is undoubtedly pearl barley. Barley does not need to be soaked, and it usually cooks in about 45 minutes. Because their cooking times are comparable, barley and brown rice can join forces in this tasty pilaf.

Serve with a topping of stir-fried vegetables for a nutritious vegetarian main dish.

1	tablespoon olive oil
½	cup chopped onion
1	cup long-grain brown or American basmati-style brown rice
½	cup barley
2	tablespoons raisins
1	stick (about 2-inch) cinnamon
2½	cups reduced-sodium or homemade chicken broth (page 75)
	Salt to taste
2	tablespoons natural (unblanched) sliced almonds

1. Heat the oil in a large (4-quart) saucepan. Add the onion and cook, stirring, over medium-low heat, until golden, about 5 minutes. Add the rice, barley, raisins and cinnamon stick; stir until the mixture is coated with the onion, about 1 minute. Add the broth; add salt to taste. Heat to boiling.

2. Stir the rice-barley mixture once; cover and cook over medium heat until the water is absorbed and the rice and barley are tender, about 55 minutes.

3. Place the almonds in a small skillet; stir constantly over low heat until they are lightly toasted, about 2 minutes.

4. Spoon the rice-barley mixture into a serving dish, remove the cinnamon stick and top with the almonds.

SWEET ORANGE BASMATI RICE

Makes 4 servings

TIP

* *Real basmati rice is imported from India and Pakistan, but there are many different hybrids of it growing in the American South.*

203 CALORIES PER SERVING

5 G PROTEIN

2 G FAT

42 G CARBOHYDRATE

27 MG SODIUM

3 MG CHOLESTEROL

UNTIL QUITE RECENTLY, the plain long-grain white rice was all most people knew. This dish is the perfect showcase for the sweet popcornlike aroma and nutty flavor of the newly popular basmati-type rice. Whereas regular long-grain has more sticky starch than dry, basmati has more dry starch than sticky. Its grains elongate and become dry and separate as they cook.

1 teaspoon unsalted butter or vegetable oil
1 strip (2-x-½-inch) orange zest (removed with a vegetable peeler), finely chopped (about 1 teaspoon)
2 teaspoons sugar
1 cup basmati rice or other long-grain white rice
1 tablespoon dried currants
1 stick (1-inch) cinnamon
1 cardamom pod, or ⅛ teaspoon ground
1 whole clove
1 slice fresh gingerroot
1¾ cups reduced-sodium or homemade chicken broth (page 75)
Salt to taste

1. Heat the butter or vegetable oil in a medium (3-quart) saucepan over very low heat. Stir in the orange zest and sugar. Cook, stirring, for 1 minute. Add the rice, currants, cinnamon stick, cardamom, clove and ginger. Stir to blend. Add the broth and salt to taste. Heat to boiling.

2. Stir the boiling rice once. Cover and cook over medium heat until the water is absorbed and the rice is tender, about 15 minutes. Let stand, uncovered, for 5 minutes. Remove the cinnamon, cardamom, clove and ginger before serving.

LEMON ORZO

Makes 4 servings

ORZO IS A SMALL RICE-SHAPED PASTA, which is generally found next to the pastina and pasta alphabets in most supermarkets. A quick-cooking alternative to rice or potatoes, it is often used in soups. It also serves as a tasty side dish. Topped with steamed vegetables, this preparation makes a delicious low-fat vegetarian main dish.

2 teaspoons butter or extra-virgin olive oil
¼ cup chopped onion
1 cup orzo (rice-shaped pasta)
1 teaspoon grated lemon zest
3 cups reduced-sodium or homemade chicken broth
   (page 75), water or half broth and half water
½ teaspoon salt, or to taste
1 tablespoon fresh lemon juice

1. Heat 1 teaspoon of the butter or olive oil in a medium (3-quart) saucepan over low heat. Add the onion and stir until the onion is tender. Add the orzo and lemon zest and continue to cook, stirring, until the orzo is well coated.

2. Add the broth and/or water and the salt; stir. Cook, uncovered, over low heat, stirring occasionally, until the orzo is tender, about 15 minutes.

3. Stir in the remaining butter and lemon juice.

TIP

✳ *Butter is used in this dish because its sweet flavor balances the acid of the lemon. Those on a low-cholesterol diet can use olive oil.*

135 CALORIES PER SERVING

5 G PROTEIN

3 G FAT

22 G CARBOHYDRATE

329 MG SODIUM

5 MG CHOLESTEROL

SOUTHWESTERN–STYLE BAKED BEANS

Makes 6 servings

* *For the quick-soak method, see page 172.*

307 CALORIES PER SERVING

16 G PROTEIN

6 G FAT

49 G CARBOHYDRATE

32 MG SODIUM

O MG CHOLESTEROL

THE FLAVORS IN THESE CONTEMPORARY BAKED BEANS are Southwestern, with garlic, spicy green chili peppers, cilantro and lime juice. Beans and grains, both touted for their reserves of complex carbohydrates, anti-carcinogenic properties and their good-quality, low-fat protein and fiber, nonetheless are sadly underemphasized in our culinary history. Yet they are simple to cook, especially if you use the foolproof oven method here.

1 pound dried pinto or Great Northern beans, rinsed and sorted

3 cups reduced-sodium or homemade chicken broth (page 75)

8 garlic cloves, bruised with the side of a knife

2 tablespoons seeded, finely chopped fresh jalapeños or other chili peppers

1 bay leaf

½ cup chopped red onion

½ cup coarsely chopped fresh cilantro

2 tablespoons olive oil

2 tablespoons fresh lime juice, or more to taste

Salt

Freshly ground black pepper

Lime wedges

1. Place the beans in a large bowl and add cold water to cover. Let stand 5 hours or overnight. Drain.

2. Preheat oven to 350 degrees F. Transfer the beans to a 2-quart casserole. Add the broth, garlic, 1 tablespoon of the jalapeño and the bay leaf. Stir to blend.

3. Cover tightly with foil and bake until the beans are tender and most of the liquid is absorbed, about 1½ hours. Uncover and let stand at room temperature until cooled.

4. Add the red onion, cilantro, olive oil, lime juice, remaining 1 tablespoon jalapeño, salt and pepper to taste. Stir to blend. Remove the bay leaf and serve with lime wedges on the side.

BARBECUE-STYLE BAKED BEANS

Makes 8 servings

REMEMBER THE CASSEROLE OF BAKED BEANS with strips of bacon dripping over the top served at every July Fourth picnic? This reduced-fat recipe uses just a single strip of bacon but lots of onion, garlic, spices, tomato, molasses and vinegar to deliver the maximum rich taste and flavor of the old-fashioned dish.

1	pound dried white kidney (cannellini), Great Northern or lima beans
3	cups reduced-sodium or homemade chicken broth (page 75)
½	onion studded with 3 whole cloves
1	bay leaf
2	garlic cloves, crushed with the side of a knife
1	tablespoon olive oil
1	cup chopped onion
1	strip lean smoky bacon, diced (¼-inch)
1	can (15 ounces) Italian-style plum tomatoes
⅓	cup dark molasses
1	tablespoon cider vinegar
½	teaspoon cayenne
½	teaspoon dried thyme leaves
¼	teaspoon dried oregano
	Salt
	Freshly ground black pepper

TIP

❋ *The soaking time for beans can be drastically reduced with the quick-soak method: Place beans in a large pot, cover with water to three times their volume and bring to a boil. Boil, uncovered, for 2 minutes; remove from the heat; cover and let sit for 1 hour. Drain and rinse well, then cook as directed in the recipe.*

231 CALORIES PER SERVING

12 G PROTEIN

3 G FAT

40 G CARBOHYDRATE

112 MG SODIUM

1 MG CHOLESTEROL

1. Place the beans in a large bowl and add cold water to cover. Let stand 5 hours or overnight. Drain.

2. Preheat oven to 350 degrees F. Transfer the beans to a 2-quart casserole. Add the chicken broth. Add clove-studded onion half to the casserole along with the bay leaf and garlic.

3. Cover tightly with foil and bake until the beans are tender and most of the liquid is absorbed, stirring once or twice during baking, about 2 hours. Remove from the oven; leave the oven on.

4. Meanwhile, heat the oil in a large (10-to-12-inch) nonstick skillet over medium-low heat; add the chopped onion and bacon; cook, stirring, until golden, about 5 minutes. Add the tomatoes, molasses, vinegar, cayenne, thyme leaves and oregano; cook, stirring, over medium heat, breaking up the tomatoes with the side of a spoon, until boiling. Lower heat and simmer, stirring occasionally, until the sauce is slightly reduced, about 10 minutes. Stir the tomato mixture into the beans.

5. Return the casserole to the oven and bake, covered, until the tomatoes are reduced and thickened and the beans are well flavored, about 45 minutes. Season to taste with salt and pepper. Remove the onion half and bay leaf before serving.

LENTILS & CARROTS

Makes 4 servings

TIP

✳ *The lentil is an excellent source of protein, with 16 grams in a cup of cooked, almost the same as in 3 ounces of beef. Unlike beef, however, lentils are also a fine source of fiber and contain no cholesterol.*

244 CALORIES PER SERVING

16 G PROTEIN

4 G FAT

38 G CARBOHYDRATE

525 MG SODIUM

0 MG CHOLESTEROL

BECAUSE TINY BUTTON-SHAPED LENTILS do not need to be soaked and usually cook in 20 to 30 minutes, they offer a degree of spontaneity not possible with other dried legumes. Serve as a side dish with lamb, chicken or seafood.

1 cup dried brown lentils, rinsed and sorted

6 cups water

1 wedge onion studded with 2 whole cloves

1 bay leaf

1 garlic clove, bruised with the side of a knife

1 tablespoon olive oil

½ cup chopped onion

½ cup diced (¼-inch) carrot

½ cup diced (¼-inch) red bell pepper

1 tablespoon peeled, finely chopped fresh gingerroot

2 teaspoons finely chopped garlic

½ cup small frozen peas, thawed

2 tablespoons reduced-sodium soy sauce

Freshly ground black pepper

1. Combine the lentils, water, clove-studded onion wedge, bay leaf and garlic in a medium (3-quart) saucepan. Heat to boiling. Cook, uncovered, over medium heat, stirring occasionally, until the lentils are tender, about 20 to 25 minutes. Do not overcook. Drain. Discard the onion wedge, garlic and bay leaf.

2. Heat the olive oil in a large (10-to-12-inch) skillet over medium heat. Add the chopped onion and carrot and cook, stirring, until tender, about 5 minutes. Stir in the red bell pepper, ginger and chopped garlic; sauté 3 minutes. Add the drained lentils, green peas, soy sauce and a grinding of black pepper. Stir just to blend. Taste and adjust seasonings and serve.

OVEN FRENCH FRIES

Makes 4 servings

I SHUDDER WHEN I THINK of all those beef-tallow fried potatoes I have consumed in the past. These crunchy oven fries are superb, more convenient to prepare and obviously more healthful than their deep-fried "French" inspiration, for they are simply tossed with a minimum of vegetable oil and allowed to oven-fry on a large baking sheet until crisp. Finely chopped parsley and garlic take the place of most of the usual salt.

1   pound russet potatoes, peeled
2   teaspoons vegetable oil
1   tablespoon coarsely chopped fresh Italian (flat-leaf) parsley
1   small garlic clove, coarsely chopped
¼   teaspoon coarse (kosher) salt

1. Preheat oven to 425 degrees F. Turn the potatoes lengthwise and cut at ½-inch-wide intervals. Cut these slices lengthwise into ½-inch-wide fries. Rinse with cold water and dry thoroughly between dishcloths.

2. Place in a large bowl; toss with the oil. Arrange in a single layer on a large nonstick baking sheet.

3. Bake until the potatoes begin to brown, about 20 minutes. Remove the baking sheet from the oven and carefully turn the potatoes. Return to the oven and bake 15 minutes.

4. Meanwhile, chop the parsley and garlic together until very fine. Sprinkle this mixture over the potatoes and bake until nicely browned, about 5 minutes more. Sprinkle with the salt and serve immediately.

TIP

❋ *Oven-frying also works as a fat-reduction technique for other foods that are traditionally deep-fried (see Oven-Roasted Eggplant, page 142, and Oven-Fried Fish Fillets, page 234).*

130 CALORIES PER SERVING

2 G PROTEIN

2 G FAT

26 G CARBOHYDRATE

124 MG SODIUM

0 MG CHOLESTEROL

SCALLOPED POTATOES

Makes 4 servings

* *The Turkish bay leaf called
for here has a mild flavor and is
not as exotic as it sounds. It is
merely the pale, gray-green bay
leaf found in jars in every
supermarket. The more pungent-
flavored California bay leaf is
very long and dark green. It is
not as readily available. If used
in this dish, the flavor would be
overwhelming.*

* *For more about fresh goat
cheese, see page 18.*

* *If using dried thyme, place it
on the wax paper with the flour,
salt and pepper in step 2.*

215 CALORIES PER SERVING

5 G PROTEIN

7 G FAT

33 G CARBOHYDRATE

261 MG SODIUM

16 MG CHOLESTEROL

SCALLOPED POTATOES ARE THE MAINSTAY of Sunday dinners, church suppers and holiday celebrations. This modified version bakes the potatoes in individual ramekins, although the recipe can be doubled and prepared in a large dish, if preferred. Vegetable oil is used instead of butter, and low-fat milk is substituted for the usual whole milk. Fresh goat cheese contributes flavor and creamy texture.

2	teaspoons olive oil
1	pound small, round, white potatoes (brown-skinned, not red), peeled
3	tablespoons finely chopped fresh parsley
1½	teaspoons chopped fresh thyme leaves, stripped from stems, or ¼ teaspoon dried
2	teaspoons all-purpose flour
¼	teaspoon salt
	Freshly ground black pepper
¼	cup crumbled fresh goat cheese (about ⅔ of a 3.5-ounce log)
2	Turkish bay leaves
¾	cup low-fat or skim milk

1. Preheat oven to 350 degrees F. Brush a 4-cup soufflé or other baking dish or four 8-ounce soufflé or pudding dishes with the olive oil. Arrange on a baking sheet. If using the small dishes, place an oiled strip of foil 1 inch wide and at least 9 inches long along the bottom and up the sides of each dish so it will be easy to loosen the potatoes and turn them out after cooking.

2. Slice the potatoes paper-thin with a sharp, thin knife or the slicing blade of a food processor. On three separate pieces of wax paper, combine the parsley and thyme; the flour, salt and pepper; and the crumbled goat cheese.

3. Place ½ of a bay leaf on the bottom of each small dish. Layer the potato slices, sprinkling some of the parsley mixture, the flour mixture and the goat cheese between each layer.

4. Pour the milk over the potatoes and cover tightly with aluminum foil. Bake the casserole 1 hour and the individual dishes 45 minutes. Remove from the oven and uncover. Bake until the top is browned and the potatoes are tender, about 30 minutes more for the casserole and about 20 minutes more for the individual dishes. Let stand about 15 minutes before serving.

5. Serve the potatoes from the casserole dish. To serve the individual scalloped potatoes, loosen the sides with the tip of a knife and carefully unmold onto the plates.

STUFFED BAKED POTATOES

Makes 4 servings

TIP

✳ *Two ounces of sour cream has 100 calories and 10 grams of fat, while low-fat cottage cheese has only 45 calories and less than 1 gram of fat.*

186 CALORIES PER SERVING

9 G PROTEIN

1 G FAT

35 G CARBOHYDRATE

145 MG SODIUM

4 MG CHOLESTEROL

YOU WON'T MISS THE UBIQUITOUS DOLLOP OF SOUR CREAM when you taste this topping of warm cottage cheese and melted mozzarella on a baked potato.

4 large baking potatoes, washed and dried
½ cup low-fat cottage cheese
¼ cup thinly sliced green scallion tops
2 tablespoons low-fat plain yogurt or skim or low-fat milk, or more to taste
Salt to taste
⅛ teaspoon freshly ground black pepper
¼ cup shredded part-skim mozzarella

1. Preheat oven to 400 degrees F. Pierce each potato with the tines of a large roasting fork or insert an aluminum baking nail (to speed baking time) lengthwise into each potato. Bake the potatoes until tender, about 50 to 60 minutes normally, or about 30 minutes when baking nails are used.

2. Split the potatoes in half lengthwise; cool slightly. Using a spoon, scoop out the potato flesh, leaving the skin intact. In a bowl, combine the potato flesh, cottage cheese, scallions, yogurt or milk, salt and black pepper. Mash together with a fork; spoon back into the potato skins. Place in a shallow baking dish and top the potatoes evenly with the shredded mozzarella.

3. Reduce oven to 350 degrees F. Return the potatoes to the oven and bake them just until the cheese melts, about 15 minutes.

MASHED POTATOES
without GUILT

Makes 4 servings

TIP

❋ *Melting the butter on top instead of mixing it in makes a little go a long way.*

283 CALORIES PER SERVING

7 G PROTEIN

7 G FAT

49 G CARBOHYDRATE

318 MG SODIUM

20 MG CHOLESTEROL

THE SECRET IS TO CUT BACK ON THE BUTTER—and thus the fat and cholesterol—without losing the rich flavor. To accomplish this, the potatoes are mashed or beaten with yogurt (for those who love its tangy flavor) or skim milk (for those who prefer a milkier taste). Then a substantially reduced amount of butter is melted and served in a small pool on top of each serving, concentrating the flavor.

2   pounds russet or baking potatoes, pared and
    cubed (½-inch), about 5 cups

1   teaspoon salt

1   cup low-fat plain yogurt or ½ cup skim milk,
    or more as needed

2   tablespoons unsalted butter, melted

1. Place the potatoes in a large saucepan; add water to cover and the salt. Heat to boiling over high heat. Reduce heat, cover and cook until tender, about 15 minutes. Drain the water and transfer the potatoes to a food mill or ricer set over the saucepan. Or, if preferred, transfer the potatoes back to the saucepan and mash them with a potato masher or a portable electric mixer.

2. Add the yogurt or the skim milk to the mashed potatoes and stir with a large spoon until blended. Spoon the potatoes onto individual plates. Drizzle ½ tablespoon of melted butter over each serving. Serve at once.

Chapter 7

MAIN DISHES

Main Dishes

The transition from the meat-and-potatoes school of meal planning began rather abruptly in my home a few years ago when I wrote a pasta cookbook. Faced with a daunting number of dishes to taste, my family and all our neighbors, who soon became the beneficiaries of my little project, fell into the pleasurable practice of eating pasta every day. It turned out to be a delicious experience. We not only enjoyed all we wanted of our favorite dishes—sometimes several at one sitting—but we somehow still managed to lose weight in the process. It was another confirmation of the benefits of a diet high in complex carbohydrates but mercifully low in fat.

Although we no longer sit down to pasta every night, the lessons of the past have had their effect, and seafood, noodles and thick soups appear on my menu at least as often as meat. One of the most effortless ways to balance one's repertoire and reduce fat naturally is to concentrate on dishes in which meat shares space with vegetables: stews, soups, pot pies, chili and the like.

At other times, I apply an elementary rule: I simply serve less meat, allotting four to five ounces per serving instead of the usual six to eight. Fatty gravies are unnecessary. Instead, I boil the juices together with wine and fresh herbs until they are lightly thickened, or I puree vegetables that have been cooked in the juices and serve them as a sauce.

I also make sure to select the leanest counterparts of my favorite cuts, substituting chicken breast for whole chicken, pork tenderloin for fatty shoulder and round of beef for chuck. Ground turkey, used in place of part or all the beef in hamburgers, meatballs or meat loaf, is just as tasty but much less fatty, and turkey cutlets make juicy stand-ins for cholesterol-rich veal.

As often as possible, I rely on moist cooking techniques like poaching, braising and stewing to keep lean cuts tender. I typically begin by cooking onions and garlic slowly in a minimum of oil, so they release rich, round flavor. The natural sweetness of bell peppers, parsnips and carrots further flavors the pot, and mushrooms, another wonder vegetable, contribute meaty taste. Fresh herbs—essentials in my kitchen—are strewn over and in everything. (I store small bunches in the refrigerator in a juice glass half filled with water and covered with an inverted sandwich bag. Some of the tough-leaved varieties, especially thyme and rosemary, will last for almost two weeks kept in this way.)

For those times when nothing but crunch will satisfy, fried food is not out of the question—fortunately. Rolling fish fillets or chicken or turkey cutlets in beaten egg white and toasted bread crumbs, then baking them in a hot oven makes them unfailingly crisp and is not only a healthier but an easier way to "fry."

For most evenings, however, give me a bowl of pasta, a sturdy vegetable dish or a bowl of chili with rice, and I'll happily call it dinner.

Vegetarian & Pasta Dishes

Chicken & Turkey

Beef & Pork

Fish

VEGETARIAN LASAGNA

Makes 8 servings

TRADITIONAL LASAGNA, LAYERED WITH RICOTTA, mozzarella and meat-based tomato sauce, is a haven for excess fat. Even vegetarian lasagna, if not carefully conceived, can be problematic. Use low-fat cheese, and to keep the flavor, don't skimp on the tomato sauce, fresh herbs and vegetables.

412 CALORIES PER SERVING

24 G PROTEIN

16 G FAT

44 G CARBOHYDRATE

577 MG SODIUM

43 MG CHOLESTEROL

½   cup finely chopped onion
2   tablespoons olive oil
2   garlic cloves, finely chopped
1   can (35 ounces) Italian-style plum tomatoes,
      crushed or pureed in a food processor
3   tablespoons chopped fresh Italian (flat-leaf) parsley
2   tablespoons chopped fresh basil (optional)
½   teaspoon salt, or to taste
      Freshly ground black pepper
2½ cups (about 8 ounces) trimmed, chopped
      well-rinsed leeks (white part only)
½   cup chopped carrot
1   teaspoon fresh thyme leaves, stripped from
      the stems, or ¼ teaspoon dried
1   package (10 ounces) white button mushrooms,
      finely chopped
1   tablespoon finely chopped sun-dried tomatoes
2   containers (15 ounces each) skim-milk ricotta
4   tablespoons grated Parmesan cheese,
      preferably Parmigiano-Reggiano
      Pinch of nutmeg
9   lasagna noodles
1   cup shredded skim-milk mozzarella

1. Combine ¼ cup of the onion and 1 teaspoon of the olive oil in a large (10-to-12-inch) nonstick skillet. Cook, stirring, over low heat until softened, about 5 minutes. Stir in 1 clove of the garlic and cook, stirring, 1 minute. Add the plum tomatoes and heat to boiling. Cook, stirring occasionally, over medium heat until the sauce is slightly thickened, about 15 minutes. Add 1 tablespoon of the parsley, 1 tablespoon of the basil (if using), the ½ teaspoon salt and a grinding of black pepper. Set aside until ready to use.

2. Combine the leeks, carrot and 2 teaspoons of the olive oil in a large (10-to-12-inch) nonstick skillet. Cook, stirring occasionally, over low heat until the leeks are tender, about 15 minutes. Add the thyme, a pinch of salt and a grinding of black pepper. Transfer to a medium bowl and reserve.

3. Combine the mushrooms and the remaining 1 tablespoon of olive oil in the skillet. Cook, stirring, over medium-low heat until the mushrooms give up some of their moisture. Add the remaining ¼ cup onion, the sun-dried tomatoes and the remaining clove of garlic. Cook, stirring, over medium-high heat until the onion is tender and the mushrooms begin to brown, about 5 minutes. Add a pinch of salt and a grinding of black pepper. Reserve.

4. In a bowl, stir the ricotta, Parmesan cheese, the remaining 2 tablespoons parsley, the remaining 1 tablespoon basil, if using, and the nutmeg until blended. Set aside.

5. Cook the lasagna noodles in boiling salted water until al dente, or firm to the bite, about 10 minutes. Drain well. Let stand in a bowl of cool water so they won't stick together. Drain before assembling the lasagna.

6. Preheat oven to 350 degrees F. Spoon about ½ cup of the tomato sauce into a 13-x-9-inch baking dish and spread evenly. Top with three of the lasagna noodles, slightly overlapping them. Stir half of the ricotta mixture into the leek mixture until blended, then spread in an even layer over the lasagna noodles. Top with ¼ cup of the mozzarella; spoon about ½ cup of the tomato sauce on top.

7. Repeat, using a second layer of three lasagna noodles, slightly overlapping one another. Stir the mushroom mixture into the remaining ricotta until blended, then spread over the noodles. Top with ¼ cup of the mozzarella, then about ½ cup of the tomato sauce.

8. Repeat, using the remaining three lasagna noodles, slightly overlapping one another. Spread the remaining tomato sauce on the top. Sprinkle with the remaining mozzarella cheese. Bake until browned and bubbly, about 45 minutes.

PASTA PRIMAVERA

Makes 6 servings

427 CALORIES PER SERVING

15 G PROTEIN

8 G FAT

76 G CARBOHYDRATE

267 MG SODIUM

2 MG CHOLESTEROL

EVERYONE LOVES PASTA WITH VEGETABLES. But often, all the healthful complex carbohydrates are negated by a rich cream-based sauce. Here, the tomato pulp is chopped and cooked with a small amount of olive oil and garlic, and lots of fresh basil is added.

2	pounds plum tomatoes, halved and cored
2	tablespoons extra-virgin olive oil
1	garlic clove, finely chopped
¼	cup packed shredded basil leaves
	Salt to taste
	Freshly ground black pepper to taste
1	pound penne, shells or other pasta shape
½	teaspoon salt, or more to taste
2	carrots, cut into 2-x-¼-inch sticks (about 1¼ cups)
8	asparagus spears, stems peeled and cut in 2-inch lengths
1	small zucchini, cut into 2-x-¼-inch sticks (about 1¼ cups)
1	yellow squash, cut into 2-x-¼-inch sticks (about 1¼ cups)
¼	pound snow peas, trimmed
½	cup thin lengthwise slivers red onion
3	tablespoons grated Parmesan cheese, preferably Parmigiano-Reggiano

1. Using a spoon, scoop the pulp, juices and seeds from the insides of the tomatoes and coarsely chop the pulp. Cut the outer shell or flesh of the tomato in ¼-inch-thick lengthwise strips; set aside separately.

2. Heat the oil in a large (10-inch) skillet over medium heat. Add the garlic and cook 1 minute. Stir in the reserved tomato pulp (about 1 cup) and cook, stirring, until it makes a smooth sauce, about 5 minutes. Add the tomato strips and basil and cook until warmed through, about 5 minutes. Remove from the heat. Season to taste with salt and pepper.

3. Meanwhile, heat a large (8-quart) saucepan of water to boiling. Add the pasta and salt to taste. Boil the pasta, stirring frequently, until it is almost cooked, 8 to 10 minutes. Add the carrots and cook 1 minute; add the asparagus and cook 1 minute; add the zucchini, yellow squash and snow peas and cook 1 minute.

4. When the vegetables and pasta are just tender, drain, reserving ½ cup of the cooking liquid. In a large serving bowl, toss together the pasta and vegetables, tomato mixture, red onion slivers, 2 tablespoons of the grated cheese and the reserved cooking water. Sprinkle with the remaining 1 tablespoon cheese.

SPINACH LINGUINE
with TOMATOES

Makes 4 servings

TIP

＊ *During tomato season, omit
the canned tomatoes and use
8 firm, ripe plum tomatoes,
halved. Ripen tomatoes in a
brown paper bag or a shaded
spot in your kitchen. Both
refrigeration and a sunny
windowsill deplete the nutrients
in underripe tomatoes.*

342 CALORIES PER SERVING

13 G PROTEIN

5 G FAT

63 G CARBOHYDRATE

262 MG SODIUM

67 MG CHOLESTEROL

LINGUINE WITH AN INTENSELY FLAVORED roasted red bell pepper sauce is a refined alternative to heavy spaghetti with meat sauce.

2 red bell peppers, seeds, stems and ribs discarded,
    cut into ½-inch strips
2 teaspoons extra-virgin olive oil
1 medium onion, halved lengthwise and sliced
1 garlic clove, bruised with the side of a knife
½ cup water
1 can (28 ounces) Italian-style plum tomatoes
½ cup low-fat or skim milk
1 sprig fresh basil, or pinch dried
1 pound fresh or dried spinach linguine or fettuccine
2 cups rinsed, trimmed, tightly packed fresh spinach leaves
    (optional)

1. Preheat oven to 400 degrees F. Combine the red peppers and oil in a large baking dish; toss to coat. Roast 20 minutes, or until the peppers begin to char. Stir in the onion, garlic and water; bake until the onion and peppers are very soft, about 25 minutes.

2. Add the tomatoes; stir to blend and to scrape up any darkened bits. Transfer to a large (10-to-12-inch) skillet and heat, stirring, to crush the tomatoes. Place the milk in a medium bowl and stir a little of the tomato-pepper mixture into the milk. Stir the mixture back into the skillet; add the basil. Heat, stirring, uncovered, over medium-low heat until the mixture boils; cook, stirring, to break up the peppers, until the sauce is chunky and thickened.

3. Cook the spinach linguine or fettuccine in boiling salted water 2 to 3 minutes for fresh or 5 to 8 minutes for dried. Just before draining, stir in the spinach, if using; drain in a colander.

4. Transfer the pasta to a large, deep platter and top with the sauce.

VEGETARIAN CHOW MEIN

Makes 4 servings

※ *Served without the noodles, this is an excellent vegetable side dish.*

338 CALORIES PER SERVING

11 G PROTEIN

5 G FAT

60 G CARBOHYDRATE

376 MG SODIUM

0 MG CHOLESTEROL

THIS CONTEMPORARY CHOW MEIN, with its mélange of fresh vegetables, is a far cry from the canned mixture once considered exotic fare. It includes fresh snow peas, shiitake mushrooms and bok choy—common ingredients that are relatively new to most supermarket produce sections—as well as carrots and red bell peppers, canned bamboo shoots and water chestnuts. The vegetables are combined with an aromatic sauce of sesame oil, reduced-sodium soy sauce and dry sherry. Served over fresh Chinese noodles or linguine, this makes a delicious vegetarian main dish.

1 pound fresh Chinese egg noodles or 8 ounces dried linguine

½ teaspoon sesame oil

Pinch of salt

1 cup trimmed snow peas (about 3 ounces)

⅓ cup reduced-sodium or homemade chicken broth (page 75)

3 tablespoons dry sherry

2 tablespoons reduced-sodium soy sauce

1 teaspoon sesame oil

2 teaspoons cornstarch

2 teaspoons vegetable oil

1 tablespoon peeled, finely chopped fresh gingerroot

2 garlic cloves, finely chopped

1 package (3.5 ounces) shiitake mushrooms, stems discarded, caps quartered, or 4 ounces white button mushrooms

2 cups diced (about ½-inch) bok choy

½ cup slivered (2-x-¼-inch pieces) carrot

½ cup slivered (2-x-¼-inch pieces) red bell pepper

1 can (6 ounces) sliced bamboo shoots, drained and rinsed

1   **can (6 ounces) sliced water chestnuts, drained and rinsed**
     Freshly ground black pepper
2   **tablespoons thin diagonal slices green scallion tops**

1. Cook the Chinese noodles in boiling salted water for 2 to 3 minutes or the linguine for 8 to 10 minutes; drain. Rinse with cold water and drain. Toss in a bowl with the ½ teaspoon sesame oil and salt; set aside.

2. Blanch the snow peas in boiling water 2 minutes and drain. Rinse with cold water; set aside.

3. In a small bowl, combine the chicken broth, sherry, soy sauce and sesame oil. Add the cornstarch and whisk until blended; set aside.

4. Heat a large (12-inch) nonstick skillet over medium heat until hot enough to evaporate a drop of water upon contact. Add the vegetable oil, ginger and garlic; stir-fry 10 seconds. Add the mushrooms and stir-fry 30 seconds.

5. Stir in the snow peas, bok choy, carrot, red bell pepper, bamboo shoots and water chestnuts. Turn the heat to high and stir-fry until the vegetables are heated through, about 3 minutes.

6. Add the broth mixture and cook, stirring, over high heat until the liquid boils and thickens slightly, about 2 minutes. Transfer half of the vegetable mixture to a side dish. Add the cooked noodles to the skillet, stir to blend and heat through, about 1 minute. Add a grinding of black pepper.

7. Transfer the noodle mixture to a serving dish. Top with the reserved vegetable mixture and sprinkle with the scallions.

186 CALORIES PER SERVING

10 G PROTEIN

10 G FAT

17 G CARBOHYDRATE

172 MG SODIUM

17 MG CHOLESTEROL

EGGPLANT PARMESAN

Makes 4 servings as a main dish or 6 servings as a side dish

BRUSHING EGGPLANT LIGHTLY with a thin film of olive oil and baking it in a hot oven until it is browned and tender works just as well as frying it, if not better. The following recipe lightens the taste of the dish considerably by using slices of fresh tomato instead of tomato sauce.

2   medium eggplants, trimmed and peeled, cut into ¼-inch-thick slices

4   teaspoons olive oil

1   garlic clove, crushed through a press

2   tablespoons julienne strips fresh basil leaves

1   tablespoon grated Parmesan cheese, preferably Parmigiano-Reggiano

2   medium firm-ripe tomatoes, peeled, cored and cut into thin slices

4   ounces part-skim mozzarella, cut into thin slices

1. Preheat oven to 425 degrees F. Arrange the eggplant in a single layer on one or two baking sheets. Stir 2 teaspoons of the olive oil and the garlic in a small bowl. Lightly brush the top sides of the eggplant slices with the oil mixture. Turn the slices over. Add the remaining 2 teaspoons oil to the bowl and lightly brush the other sides of the eggplant. Bake until the bottom sides are lightly browned, about 15 minutes. Turn the eggplant slices and bake until tender and golden, 10 to 15 minutes longer. Cool on a rack.

2. Reduce oven temperature to 350 degrees F. In a 11-x-7-inch oval or 8-inch round baking dish, arrange half the eggplant slices, slightly overlapping. Top with half the basil and 1 teaspoon of the Parmesan cheese. Arrange the tomatoes, slightly overlapping, in a solid layer on top of the eggplant. Top the tomatoes with the remaining basil, half of the mozzarella and 1 teaspoon of the Parmesan. Add the remaining eggplant slices, slightly overlapping; top with the remaining mozzarella and the remaining 1 teaspoon of the Parmesan.

3. Cover with foil and bake 30 minutes. Remove the foil and bake until the mozzarella is golden and bubbly, about 10 minutes longer. Cool slightly before serving.

BELL PEPPERS STUFFED with ORZO

Makes 4 servings

I NEVER LIKED STUFFED BELL PEPPERS, with their gray lumps of meat sitting in waterlogged, wrinkled skins. Roasted peppers, however, offer a vast improvement over the original, particularly when stuffed with orzo, a small rice-shaped pasta found in the pasta section of most supermarkets.

4	medium red or green bell peppers
3	teaspoons olive oil
1	garlic clove, bruised with the side of a knife
	Salt
	Freshly ground black pepper
1	cup uncooked orzo or other small pasta shape
½	cup chopped onion
2	tablespoons finely chopped prosciutto or other cured ham
½	cup fresh or frozen tiny green peas
½	cup diced, seeded tomato
4	tablespoons grated Parmesan cheese, preferably Parmigiano-Reggiano
2	tablespoons chopped fresh basil leaves
1	tablespoon pine nuts (pignoli), toasted in a dry skillet for 1 minute (optional)
1	large egg, beaten

1. Preheat oven to 400 degrees F. Cut the tops off the peppers; carefully cut out the seeds and ribs. Brush the outside of the peppers lightly with 1 teaspoon of the olive oil. Place the peppers on their sides in a 10-inch square or 1½-quart baking dish; add the garlic to the bottom of the baking dish. Roast, turning often, until the peppers begin to char but are still firm, about 20 minutes.

2. Remove from oven; arrange the peppers open ends up; sprinkle the insides with a little salt and a grinding of black pepper; cool slightly. Reduce oven temperature to 350 degrees F.

3. Meanwhile, cook the orzo in plenty of boiling salted water, uncovered, until tender, about 12 minutes. Drain, rinse with cool water and set aside. There should be 2 cups cooked orzo.

4. Combine the remaining 2 teaspoons of olive oil and the onion in a large (10-inch) nonstick skillet; cook, stirring, over low heat until soft, about 5 minutes. Add the prosciutto or ham and cook 3 minutes. Remove from the heat. Add the cooked orzo, peas, tomato, 3 tablespoons of the cheese, the basil and the toasted pine nuts, if using; stir to blend. Add the egg and a generous grinding of black pepper.

5. Carefully spoon the orzo mixture into the partially roasted peppers, dividing it evenly and pressing down with the back of a spoon. Stand the peppers upright in the baking dish. Sprinkle the tops with the remaining 1 tablespoon cheese.

6. Bake until the tops are browned, about 30 minutes. Serve hot, warm or at room temperature.

233 CALORIES PER SERVING

11 G PROTEIN

7 G FAT

31 G CARBOHYDRATE

239 MG SODIUM

61 MG CHOLESTEROL

BLACK BEAN CHILI
with YELLOW RICE
Makes 8 servings

* *The chili is also good on its own without the rice.*

* *You can reduce the soaking time for the beans by placing them in water three times their volume and boiling, uncovered, for 2 minutes. Remove from the heat and let sit, covered, for 1 hour. Drain, rinse and proceed with the recipe. While this method does save time, the long-soaking method is preferable because it helps purge the beans of their gas-producing sugars.*

* *If you are using the Strained Yogurt topping (page 201), make it the night before.*

* *One cup canned plum tomatoes, chopped and drained, may be substituted for fresh; frozen corn may be substituted for fresh.*

LEAVING THE MEAT OUT of the traditional red bean chili removes much of the fat but also steals most of the roundness and flavor from the dish. In place of meat, this chili uses black beans, which are infinitely richer and fuller-tasting than the red variety. The robust result is stunning enough to be a party dish. The chili is studded with brightly colored chunks of zucchini, yellow squash and corn. Serve it on a bed of bright yellow rice and top with a spoonful of yogurt and a sprinkling of cilantro leaves.

2   cups dried black beans, rinsed and sorted
1   tablespoon vegetable oil
1   cup chopped onion
1   cup diced (¼-inch) carrot
½   cup chopped red bell pepper
½   cup chopped green bell pepper
3   garlic cloves, finely chopped (about 1 tablespoon)
2   tablespoons chili powder
2   teaspoons ground cumin
½   teaspoon cayenne pepper
1   bay leaf
6   cups water
1   cup chopped cored plum tomatoes
1   teaspoon salt, or to taste
1   cup diced (¼-inch) zucchini
1   cup diced (¼-inch) yellow squash
½   cup corn kernels cut from the cob
1   tablespoon seeded, finely chopped jalapeño peppers,
      or more to taste

Yellow Rice (page 200)
Strained Yogurt (optional, page 201)
¼ **cup chopped fresh cilantro**

178 CALORIES PER SERVING

9 G PROTEIN

3 G FAT

31 G CARBOHYDRATE

354 MG SODIUM

0 MG CHOLESTEROL

1. Place the beans in a large bowl and cover with cold water. Let stand at least 4 hours or overnight. Drain.

2. Heat the oil in a large (5-quart) saucepan over medium heat. Add the onion and cook, stirring, until it is soft, about 5 minutes. Add the carrot, red and green bell peppers, garlic, chili powder, cumin, cayenne and bay leaf. Continue cooking, stirring often, until the vegetables are soft, about 10 minutes.

3. Add the black beans and the 6 cups water. Bring to a boil, reduce heat, cover and simmer 1 hour. Add the tomatoes and salt; cook, uncovered, until the beans are tender and the mixture is thick, 45 to 60 minutes.

4. Add the zucchini, yellow squash, corn and jalapeños; cook just until the vegetables are tender, about 10 minutes. Taste and adjust the seasonings.

5. To serve, ladle onto a bed of Yellow Rice. Serve topped with a spoonful of Strained Yogurt, if using, and a sprinkling of chopped cilantro.

YELLOW RICE

Makes 8 servings

129 CALORIES PER SERVING

3 G PROTEIN

0 G FAT

28 G CARBOHYDRATE

138 MG SODIUM

0 MG CHOLESTEROL

1 teaspoon ground turmeric
½ teaspoon ground cumin
2¾ cups water
1½ cups long-grain white rice
½ teaspoon salt
½ cup thinly sliced green scallion tops

1. Place the turmeric and cumin in a large (4-quart) saucepan. Turn heat to low and heat the spices, stirring constantly, just until fragrant, about 30 seconds.

2. Add the water, rice and salt and heat to boiling. Cover and cook over low heat until the liquid is absorbed and the rice is tender, about 15 minutes. Let stand, covered, 5 minutes. Do not stir.

3. To serve, spoon into a serving bowl and sprinkle with the sliced scallion tops.

STRAINED YOGURT

Makes about ¾ cup

YOGURT LEFT TO DRAIN in a cheesecloth-lined sieve overnight thickens to the consistency of crème fraîche. If allowed to stand even longer, it can become a soft spread. Use it as suggested as a topping for chili or try it as a dip for vegetables; with sugar as a topping on cake or fruit; or as a substitute for mayonnaise in egg or tuna salad.

1   cup low-fat plain yogurt

Place the yogurt in a sieve and set over a bowl. Cover with plastic wrap and refrigerate 6 hours or overnight. The next day, discard the liquid in the bowl. Wipe out the bowl and add the strained yogurt. Stir until smooth.

* *Yogurts that are thickened with vegetable gums do not make good yogurt cheese because the gums tend to hold the whey in the yogurt and prevent it from draining.*

* *Letting the yogurt stand at room temperature for ½ hour before refrigerating it will hasten the draining.*

I7 CALORIES PER TABLESPOON

2 G PROTEIN

0.5 G FAT

2 G CARBOHYDRATE

I7 MG SODIUM

2 MG CHOLESTEROL

STEAMED MARINATED CHICKEN BREASTS

Makes 4 servings

TIP

✳ *Yellow and green bell peppers and thin carrot sticks and/or green beans may be added to the poaching broth and served over the chicken as well.*

164 CALORIES PER SERVING

28 G PROTEIN

3 G FAT

5 G CARBOHYDRATE

91 MG SODIUM

73 MG CHOLESTEROL.

ROASTING CHICKEN IS POPULAR, but poaching is an even better method of reducing fat. Here, boneless, skinless chicken breasts are poached and served in a light vinaigrette made with the leftover broth, vinegar and lime juice. Red bell peppers are cooked in the poaching liquid until crisp-tender and served over the thin-sliced chicken. This is a delicious main dish with no added fat.

1	cup water
2	celery leaves
1	wedge onion
1	bay leaf
1	garlic clove, bruised with the side of a knife
1	leafy sprig fresh thyme, or pinch dried
1	leafy sprig fresh Italian (flat-leaf) parsley
1	leafy sprig fresh basil, or pinch dried
4	skinless, boneless chicken breast halves (about 6 ounces each)
1	large red bell pepper, halved, seeds, stem and inside ribs removed, cut into thin lengthwise strips
½	cup thin strips red onion, cut lengthwise
½	cup thin diagonal slices celery
3	tablespoons white-wine vinegar, or more to taste
2	tablespoons coarsely chopped fresh Italian (flat-leaf) parsley
2	tablespoons coarsely chopped fresh basil (optional)
1	teaspoon fresh thyme leaves, stripped from stems, or ¼ teaspoon dried
	Salt
	Freshly ground black pepper
1	teaspoon seeded, finely chopped jalapeño pepper (optional)

1 tablespoon fresh lime juice, or more to taste
4 thin slices lime

1. Combine the water, celery leaves, onion, bay leaf, garlic, thyme, parsley and basil in a large (10-to-12-inch) skillet with a tight-fitting lid; heat to boiling. Add the chicken breasts. Cover and cook, over medium heat, turning once, until cooked through, about 8 minutes. Transfer the chicken to a platter. Strain the broth and return it to the skillet.

2. Add the red bell pepper to the broth. Cover and cook until crisp-tender, about 3 minutes. Uncover and stir in the red onion, celery, vinegar, parsley, basil (if using), thyme, a pinch of salt and a grinding of black pepper. Cook, uncovered, stirring, 1 minute. Remove from heat.

3. Cut the chicken into ¼-inch crosswise slices and arrange them on a platter, overlapping them slightly. Spoon the broth and vegetables over the chicken. Sprinkle with the jalapeño, if using, and the lime juice. Garnish the platter with the lime slices. Serve either warm, at room temperature or chilled.

COUNTRY CAPTAIN

Makes 6 servings

TIP

✳ *To shorten the preparation time, make the sauce a few hours ahead or the night before.*

340 CALORIES PER SERVING

30 G PROTEIN

7 G FAT

38 G CARBOHYDRATE

353 MG SODIUM

69 MG CHOLESTEROL

COUNTRY CAPTAIN IS A CURRIED CHICKEN DISH popular in the American South. Traditionally, it is made from a slow-cooked stewing hen served off the bone on a bed of rice, topped with a rich curry-flavored tomato sauce studded with raisins. This version uses related ingredients but in a reduced-fat, less stewlike presentation. Because skinless, boneless chicken cutlets cook more quickly and are easier to handle and much lower in fat, I have used them instead of a whole chicken. The slightly more nutritious brown basmati rice with the bran layer intact replaces the usual white rice.

Curried Tomato Sauce

1	teaspoon olive oil
½	cup chopped onion
1	garlic clove, finely chopped
2	teaspoons good-quality curry powder
	Pinch of ground cloves
1	can (28 ounces) imported Italian-style plum tomatoes
1	bay leaf
⅛	teaspoon cayenne pepper
¼	teaspoon salt
	Freshly ground black pepper

Rice

1	teaspoon oil
1	cup brown American basmati-type rice
⅓	cup dried currants
½	garlic clove, crushed through a press
1¾	cups reduced-sodium or homemade chicken broth (page 75)
½	teaspoon salt (optional)

1   tablespoon sliced natural (unblanched) almonds

1   teaspoon olive oil

1   green bell pepper, cut into ¼-inch-long strips,
      inside ribs trimmed

6   chicken cutlets (about 6 ounces each)

1   teaspoon fresh thyme leaves, or ¼ teaspoon dried

1. **Making the sauce:** Combine the olive oil and onion in a large (10-to-12-inch) nonstick skillet. Cover and cook over low heat until the onion is tender but not browned, about 5 minutes. Uncover, stir in the garlic and cook 30 seconds. Stir in the curry and cloves until blended. Add the tomatoes; break up with the side of a spoon. Heat to boiling; add the bay leaf and cayenne. Cook, covered, over low heat for 15 minutes. Uncover and simmer until the sauce is thickened, about 15 minutes. Season to taste with salt and coarsely ground black pepper. Set aside.

2. **Meanwhile, prepare the rice:** Combine the oil and rice in a large (4-quart) saucepan. Cook over low heat, stirring, until the rice begins to turn opaque; stir in the currants and the garlic. Add the broth and salt, if using; heat to boiling; stir thoroughly. Cook, covered, over low heat until the liquid is absorbed and the rice is tender, about 15 minutes. Let the rice stand, off the heat, until ready to serve.

3. Sprinkle the almonds in a large nonstick skillet and toast, stirring constantly, over low heat, until golden, about 2 minutes. Transfer to a side dish. Add the olive oil to the skillet and heat over medium-high heat. Add the green pepper and stir-fry until the edges of the peppers are black and they are crisp-tender, about 3 minutes. Transfer to side dish. Add the chicken cutlets and cook, turning once, until browned outside, about 5 minutes. Stir in the tomato sauce and cook over low heat for 5 minutes. Remove the bay leaf from the sauce.

4. To serve, spoon the rice onto a platter. Top with the chicken cutlets and spoon the sauce over the top. Add the seared peppers; sprinkle with the toasted almonds and thyme.

OVEN-ROASTED CHICKEN BREASTS *with* LEMON & THYME

Makes 4 servings

* *For a wonderful summer dish, use 1 tablespoon packed julienne-cut fresh basil leaves instead of the fresh thyme.*

166 CALORIES PER SERVING

25 G PROTEIN

6 G FAT

I G CARBOHYDRATE

126 MG SODIUM

69 MG CHOLESTEROL

A BASIC ROAST CHICKEN is the mainstay of almost every cook's weekly repertoire. More people are turning to chicken breasts instead of whole chicken because they cook quickly and are lower in fat than thighs and legs. Here, chicken breasts are roasted in a hot oven for a short time. Watch them carefully: without the skin, they become dry if overcooked.

1 tablespoon extra-virgin olive oil

1 garlic clove, crushed through a press
Pinch of salt
Freshly ground black pepper

4 large boneless, skinless chicken breast halves
(about 1½ pounds total)

1 teaspoon fresh thyme leaves, stripped from the stems,
or ¼ teaspoon dried

4 thin slices lemon

1. Preheat oven to 400 degrees F. Combine the oil, garlic, salt and pepper in a shallow baking dish. Add the chicken and turn in the oil until coated. Arrange smooth side down and sprinkle with half of the thyme. Arrange the lemon slices around the chicken.

2. Bake the chicken 8 minutes. Turn the chicken smooth side up. Place a lemon slice on each piece of the chicken and sprinkle with the remaining thyme. Bake until the center is no longer pink, 8 to 10 minutes. Do not overcook. Serve warm or at room temperature with the pan juices spooned on top.

CHICKEN POT PIE *with* CORNMEAL BISCUIT TOPPING

Makes 6 servings

CLASSIC CHICKEN POT PIE can be a fat-laden mixture of cream sauce, chicken and vegetables encased in a rich top and bottom crust made with butter or margarine. In this lightened version, the topping has become an easy-to-make cornmeal and buttermilk biscuit topping that uses polyunsaturated vegetable oil. The filling, a mixture of lean, skinless chicken and lots of fresh vegetables, is sauced with a puree of low-fat milk and mashed potatoes laced with an assortment of fresh-tasting herbs: parsley, dill and thyme.

1	cup water
1	thick slice onion
1	leafy celery top
1	bay leaf
½	teaspoon salt
4	chicken thighs (about 12 ounces), skin removed and fat trimmed
1	whole chicken breast (about 10 ounces), skin removed and fat trimmed
2	cups peeled, diced potatoes
½	cup low-fat milk
2	teaspoons olive oil
½	cup chopped onion
1	cup sliced (about ¼-inch) carrots
1	cup trimmed, cut (about ½-inch lengths) fresh green beans
1	garlic clove, finely chopped
1	cup trimmed, cubed (½-inch) yellow squash

TIP

✴ *Buttermilk, made from skim milk, has a creamy, thick consistency that makes it ideal for baking because it mimics the properties of fat and holds in the liquid, rendering baked goods moist.*

474 CALORIES PER SERVING

24 G PROTEIN

16 G FAT

60 G CARBOHYDRATE

581 MG SODIUM

44 MG CHOLESTEROL

1   cup fresh or frozen corn kernels

½   cup fresh or frozen tiny green peas

¼   chopped fresh Italian (flat-leaf) parsley

1   tablespoon chopped fresh dill

1   teaspoon fresh thyme leaves, or pinch dried

    Salt

    Freshly ground black pepper

Cornmeal Biscuit Topping

1½   cups all-purpose flour

½   cup yellow cornmeal

2   tablespoons minced fresh chives or
     thinly sliced green scallion tops

1   tablespoon baking powder

¾   teaspoon baking soda

½   teaspoon salt

1   cup buttermilk

¼   cup vegetable oil

1   white from extra-large or large egg

1. Combine the water, onion slice, celery top, bay leaf and salt in a large (6-quart) saucepan or deep skillet with a tight-fitting lid. Heat to boiling; cover and simmer over low heat 10 minutes. Add the chicken thighs and breast. Cover and cook over medium heat, turning once, until cooked through, about 15 minutes. Uncover and let cool in the broth.

2. When cool, remove the chicken meat from the bones in large pieces. Strain the broth and reserve. Cut the chicken meat into 1-inch cubes and place in a bowl.

3. Transfer the broth to a medium (3-quart) saucepan, add the potatoes and cook, covered, over medium heat until tender, about 10 minutes. Cool slightly and transfer the potatoes and the liquid to the bowl of a food processor. Process until smooth. Gradually add the milk and process until well blended. Reserve.

4. In a large (10-to-12-inch) skillet, combine the oil and chopped onion; cook, stirring, over low heat, until tender but not brown, about 5 minutes. Add the carrots and green beans; cook, stirring occasionally, for 5 minutes, or until the vegetables are crisp-tender. Stir in the garlic; sauté 1 minute. Add the squash, corn and peas; cover and cook over low heat until the vegetables are tender, about 5 minutes.

5. Combine the cooked chicken, vegetables, potato and broth mixture, parsley, dill and thyme and season with salt and pepper to taste.

6. Preheat oven to 400 degrees F. Pour chicken mixture into six individual (about 10-ounce) casserole dishes or a large (1½-to-2-quart) casserole, soufflé dish or pie plate.

7. **Making the topping:** Stir together the flour, cornmeal, chives or scallions, baking powder, baking soda and salt. In a separate bowl, whisk the buttermilk, vegetable oil and egg white until blended. Add to the flour mixture and fold just until blended. Drop by spoonfuls onto the chicken mixture, dividing evenly. Bake until browned, 20 to 25 minutes.

STUFFED CABBAGE *with* TOMATO & DILL SAUCE

Makes 6 to 8 servings

THIS RECIPE TAKES THE EXTRA FAT and labor out of a family classic: stuffed cabbage rolls. Ground turkey, the lean alternative to beef and pork, cuts the saturated-fat calories. Instead of filling and rolling individual cabbage leaves, line a casserole with the whole blanched leaves and fill with the stuffing. The final dish, a neat dome of cabbage, is cut into wedges and served with a fresh-tasting tomato sauce laced with dill.

1	medium head green cabbage (about 1¾ pounds), preferably Savoy
1	pound ground turkey
2	cups finely chopped onion
2	teaspoons vegetable oil
½	cup chopped carrot
1	teaspoon finely chopped garlic
¼	cup chopped fresh dill
2	teaspoons grated lemon zest
1	teaspoon salt
¼	teaspoon freshly ground black pepper
	Vegetable-oil cooking spray
1	large egg
1	egg white
2-2½	cups cooked long-grain brown or white rice or short-grain brown
¼	cup fresh lemon juice
	Tomato & Dill Sauce (page 212)

1. Heat a large (6-quart) saucepan half filled with water to boiling. Add the cab-

bage, cover and simmer 5 minutes. Remove cabbage from the water to a colander and let stand until cool enough to handle. Cut the core from the cabbage, carefully peel off about 8 of the large outside leaves and reserve. Chop enough of the remaining cabbage to equal 3 cups. Reserve the remaining cabbage for another use.

2. Heat a large (10-to-12-inch) nonstick skillet over medium-high heat. Add the turkey and cook, stirring to break up the pieces, until evenly browned, about 5 minutes. Transfer turkey to a side dish and reserve.

3. Combine the onion and oil in the skillet. Cover and cook over low heat until the onion is tender, about 5 minutes. Add the carrot and garlic and sauté, stirring, over medium heat, for 5 minutes. Add the browned turkey meat, reserved chopped cabbage, dill, lemon zest, salt and pepper. Cook, stirring, frequently, until the cabbage is wilted, about 5 minutes. Cool the mixture.

4. Preheat oven to 350 degrees F. Spray a 1½-to-2 quart ovenproof casserole or bowl with vegetable-oil cooking spray. Trim the thick rib from the reserved blanched whole cabbage leaves so that it is almost flush with the rest of the leaf. Line the casserole or bowl with the leaves, reserving 1 or 2 to place on top of the filling. Set aside.

5. Beat the egg and egg white until blended. Add the cooked rice, lemon juice and the beaten egg mixture to the cooled turkey mixture. Spoon into the bowl lined with cabbage leaves. Fold the overlapping leaves over the filling and cover the top with the reserved whole leaves. Brush a coating of oil on a sheet of aluminum foil and cover the casserole with the foil, oiled side down.

6. Bake, covered, for 50 to 60 minutes, or until the cabbage appears to be well-browned. Cool about 15 minutes so that the filling can reabsorb any liquid in the bottom of the casserole. Then cover the casserole with a platter and carefully invert the stuffed cabbage onto it. Cut into wedges and serve with the Tomato & Dill Sauce.

TOMATO & DILL SAUCE

Makes about 2 cups

36 CALORIES PER SERVING

I G PROTEIN

I G FAT

6 G CARBOHYDRATE

394 MG SODIUM

O MG CHOLESTEROL

THIS SIMPLE TOMATO SAUCE is also good over grilled or poached chicken or cooked rice. Without the orange and lemon zests, it makes a tasty sauce for pasta, seasoned with basil, oregano and/or thyme instead of dill.

2 tablespoons finely chopped onion
1 tablespoon water
1 teaspoon olive oil
1 garlic clove, crushed through a press
1 can (28 ounces) Italian-style plum tomatoes with juices
2 tablespoons finely chopped fresh dill
2 tablespoons finely chopped fresh Italian (flat-leaf) parsley
1 teaspoon finely grated orange zest
½ teaspoon finely grated lemon zest
½ teaspoon salt
½ teaspoon sugar (optional)
 Freshly ground black pepper

1. Combine the onion, water and olive oil in a large (12-inch) nonstick skillet with a cover. Cook, covered, over low heat, until the onion is tender, about 5 minutes. Uncover, add the garlic and cook, stirring, over medium-low heat for 2 minutes.

2. Add the tomatoes. Cook over medium heat, stirring and breaking up the tomatoes with the side of a spoon, until the sauce is reduced and thickened, about 25 minutes. Stir in the dill, parsley, orange and lemon zests, salt and sugar, if using. Season to taste with freshly ground black pepper.

TURKEY MEAT LOAF
with ASPARAGUS &
YOGURT–MUSTARD SAUCE

Makes 8 to 10 servings

WITH A LITTLE CREATIVE SUBSTITUTION, meat loaf can be rendered lower in fat and, equally important, superior in taste and texture. The modifications include using lower-fat meats and a greater ratio of vegetables and grains to meat and selecting apt flavorings. In this version, I use ground turkey, loads of vegetables—asparagus, leeks, carrots and zucchini—and cooked white rice.

8	slender asparagus spears, trimmed and washed
1	cup finely chopped white part of well-rinsed leek
1	teaspoon olive oil
3	tablespoons water
½	cup coarsely shredded carrot
½	cup coarsely shredded zucchini
1	garlic clove, finely chopped
1	cup cooked long-grain white rice
1¾	pounds lean ground turkey
1	egg white, whisked until frothy
1	teaspoon plus 1 tablespoon grainy Dijon-style mustard
1	teaspoon salt
	Freshly ground black pepper
	Pinch of ground nutmeg
½	cup reduced-sodium or homemade chicken broth (page 75)
	Yogurt-Mustard Sauce (optional, page 215)

1. Heat 1 inch of water in a large (10-to-12-inch) skillet. Add the asparagus, cover and cook 3 minutes, or until tender; drain and set aside.

TIPS

❋ *Ground turkey is moist, juicy and much lighter in calories, fat and taste than ground red meat. Choosing it saves almost 25 percent in fat, for it contains about 12 grams of fat per serving compared with 16 grams in lean beef and 20 grams in regular beef.*

❋ *Do not overbake the loaf or it will become dry. It's essential to let lean meat loaf stand so that the juices can be reabsorbed by the meat.*

❋ *Serve leftovers cold with Yogurt-Mustard Sauce and cornichons (small, tart pickles).*

182 CALORIES PER SERVING

15 G PROTEIN

8 G FAT

11 G CARBOHYDRATE

361 MG SODIUM

37 MG CHOLESTEROL

2. Place the leek, oil and water in the skillet, cover and cook over low heat, stirring occasionally, until tender, 12 to 15 minutes. Add the carrot, zucchini and garlic and cook, stirring, for 2 minutes. Stir in the rice until blended; set aside.

3. In a large bowl, combine the turkey, egg white, 1 teaspoon mustard, salt, pepper and nutmeg. Add the rice mixture. Stir until well blended. Stir in the chicken broth until blended.

4. Preheat oven to 350 degrees F. Spoon one-third of the turkey mixture into a 9-x-5-x-2¾-inch glass loaf pan; smooth with a rubber spatula. Arrange half of the asparagus, lengthwise and evenly spaced, on top of the layer of turkey mixture. Top with another third of the turkey mixture; smooth with a spatula. Top with the remaining asparagus, spacing evenly. Add the remaining turkey mixture; smooth with a spatula. Spread the remaining 1 tablespoon of the mustard in a smooth layer on the top of the turkey loaf.

5. Bake for 1 hour 15 minutes, or until the loaf springs back when the top is pressed with a fingertip. Let stand 15 minutes so that the juices in the baking dish can be reabsorbed by the turkey loaf. Then loosen the sides of the pan; remove any milky residue that may have collected along the edges. Turn the loaf out onto a platter.

6. Using a serrated knife, carefully cut the loaf into ½-inch-thick slices. Serve hot with Yogurt-Mustard Sauce, if desired.

YOGURT-MUSTARD SAUCE

THIS YOGURT AND MUSTARD MIXTURE, a substitute for mayonnaise, is also a great dip for raw vegetables.

1 cup low-fat or nonfat plain yogurt
2 teaspoons prepared Dijon-style mustard, or more to taste
Freshly ground black pepper to taste

1. Place the yogurt in a small strainer and place over a small bowl. Cover and refrigerate overnight. The next day, discard the liquid left in the bowl.

2. In a small bowl, combine the yogurt and mustard. Add the black pepper to taste. Serve with Turkey Meat Loaf with Asparagus (page 213), if desired.

* *Compare the fat levels of mayonnaise and yogurt: mayonnaise contains about 11 grams per tablespoon, while low-fat yogurt contains a mere 0.2 grams.*

* *For more on Strained Yogurt, see the note on page 201.*

24 CALORIES PER SERVING

2 G PROTEIN

1 G FAT

2 G CARBOHYDRATE

40 MG SODIUM

3 MG CHOLESTEROL

OVEN-BAKED TURKEY CUTLET PARMESAN

Makes 4 servings

STREAMLINING THE EGG-DIPPED, oil-fried veal cutlet that is topped with a thick tomato-and-meat sauce and melted mozzarella was a fat sleuth's dream. I substitute lower-fat turkey cutlets for the veal. The egg wash is prepared with just the white, leaving the fatty egg yolk behind. The sauce is a meat-free mixture of oven-roasted vegetables, and the quantity of cheese, grated Parmigiano-Reggiano, has been "stretched" by adding it to the bread crumb mixture.

Roasted Vegetable Sauce

1   red bell pepper, halved, seeds, stem and ribs removed, cut into ½-inch-wide strips

1   yellow bell pepper, halved, seeds, stem and ribs removed, cut into ½-inch-wide strips

1   green bell pepper, halved, seeds, stem and ribs removed, cut into ½-inch-wide strips

1   cup thin onion wedges

2   garlic cloves, bruised with the side of a knife

1   tablespoon olive oil

2   cups halved cherry tomatoes or quartered plum tomatoes

1   tablespoon chopped fresh Italian (flat-leaf) parsley
    Salt
    Freshly ground black pepper

Turkey Cutlets

½   cup all-purpose flour

¼   teaspoon salt
    Freshly ground black pepper

2   egg whites

1   **cup fine dry bread crumbs**

¼   **cup grated Parmesan cheese, preferably Parmigiano-Reggiano**

1   **teaspoon snipped fresh rosemary leaves, or ½ teaspoon crumbled dried**

1   **pound thinly sliced turkey cutlets**

1. **Making the sauce:** Preheat oven to 400 degrees F. Combine the peppers, onion and garlic in a large baking dish; drizzle with the olive oil. Roast the vegetables, stirring occasionally, for 30 minutes, or until charred on the edges. Add the tomatoes; roast until they are tender and lightly browned, about 25 minutes. Season with the parsley, a sprinkling of salt and a grinding of black pepper. (The sauce can be made ahead and reheated in a skillet before serving.)

2. **Making the cutlets:** Place the flour, ¼ teaspoon salt and a grinding of black pepper on a large sheet of wax paper. Whisk the egg whites in a shallow soup bowl or pie plate until foamy. Place the bread crumbs, cheese and rosemary on another sheet of wax paper and stir to blend.

3. Roll the cutlets in the flour to coat evenly; shake off the excess. Dip them into the beaten egg whites. Roll in the bread crumbs, pressing with your fingertips to coat the cutlets evenly.

4. Preheat oven to 400 degrees F. Brush a nonstick baking sheet with a thin film of olive oil. Arrange the breaded cutlets on the prepared baking sheet and bake on the lowest oven rack for 3 minutes. Remove the pan from the oven and, using a wide spatula, turn the cutlets over. Bake until golden and crisp, about 3 minutes more.

5. Serve the cutlets topped with the warmed Roasted Vegetable Sauce.

MEAT LOAF *with* LENTILS & SPINACH

Makes 8 to 10 servings

THIS MEAT LOAF CONTAINS HALF the usual amount of ground beef. It is "beefed up" with fiber-rich lentils, lots of garlic, ginger and colorful vegetables and a dash of soy sauce. The fat and cholesterol are further lowered by using an egg white instead of a whole egg to bind the mixture.

½	cup dried brown lentils, rinsed and sorted
2	teaspoons vegetable oil
½	cup chopped onion
½	cup chopped red bell pepper
2	garlic cloves, finely chopped
1	tablespoon peeled, finely chopped fresh gingerroot
4	cups rinsed, trimmed, chopped packed fresh spinach leaves
3	tablespoons reduced-sodium soy sauce
1-1¼	pounds ground meat mixture (usually half beef, one-quarter pork and one-quarter veal)
1	egg white, beaten until frothy
½	teaspoon salt
⅛	teaspoon freshly ground black pepper

1. Cook the lentils in plenty of boiling water until tender, about 15 minutes. Drain (there should be about 1½ cups); set aside.

2. Heat the oil in a large (10-to-12-inch) nonstick skillet. Add the onion and red bell pepper and cook, stirring, until the onion is golden, about 10 minutes. Stir in the garlic and ginger; sauté 1 minute.

3. Add the spinach, cooked lentils and 2 tablespoons of the soy sauce; stir to blend. Cover and cook over medium-low heat until the spinach is wilted, about 5 minutes. Uncover and cool slightly.

4. In a large bowl, combine the meat mixture, lentil and vegetable mixture, egg white, salt and pepper. Stir until well blended.

5. Preheat oven to 350 degrees F. Spread the meat loaf in a 9-x-5-x-2¾-inch loaf pan; brush the remaining 1 tablespoon soy sauce over the top of the meat loaf. Bake until the meat loaf has pulled away from the sides of the pan and the top is well browned, about 1 hour 15 minutes. Remove from oven and let stand until almost all the juices in the pan have been reabsorbed into the meat loaf, about 15 minutes. Cut into slices and serve.

TIPS

✳ *If you can't find cremini or shiitake mushrooms, use 3 cups white button mushrooms in all.*

✳ *This recipe demonstrates how to concoct a flavorful, fast sauce using broth and wine but no butter: First the meat is seared in the skillet so that the browned bits become the flavor base; then the broth is added and reduced by boiling; and finally the wine is added and the sauce is intensified by boiling again.*

288 CALORIES PER SERVING

31 G PROTEIN

8 G FAT

18 G CARBOHYDRATE

193 MG SODIUM

72 MG CHOLESTEROL

PEPPER STEAK SANDWICH

Makes 4 servings

HOT ROAST BEEF SANDWICHES are usually made with well-marbled beef cut in thin slices and piled indiscriminately on plain white toast. Often served with mashed potatoes, they are then topped with a brown gravy made with the roast drippings. In this diplomatic approach to eating beef, a modest serving of thin slices of lean beef, coated with crushed pepper, is bolstered by a generous portion of meaty-tasting mushrooms.

2   tablespoons chopped fresh Italian (flat-leaf) parsley
1   tablespoon snipped chives or chopped green scallion tops
1   teaspoon fresh thyme leaves, stripped from the stems, or pinch dried
½   garlic clove, chopped
1   teaspoon olive oil
2   cups sliced (¼-inch) cremini or white button mushrooms
1   package (3.5 ounces) shiitake mushrooms, stems removed, caps sliced ¼ inch thick
1   tablespoon water
    Salt
1   tablespoon whole peppercorns, or less to taste
    Pinch of allspice
1   1-pound piece well-trimmed top round or flank steak
½   cup reduced-sodium or homemade beef broth (page 76)
½   cup dry red wine
4   thin slices bread, toasted

1. Finely chop the parsley, chives or scallions, thyme and garlic together; set aside.

2. Heat the oil in a large (10-inch) nonstick skillet until hot enough to sizzle a slice of mushroom. Add the mushrooms all at once and stir to coat; add the water. Cover and cook over low heat until tender, about 5 minutes. Uncover and cook over high heat until the moisture is evaporated and the mushrooms begin to brown. Stir in the parsley mixture just until blended; sprinkle with salt and transfer to a side dish. Wipe out the skillet and reserve.

3. Coarsely crack the peppercorns with a mortar and pestle or place in a small heavy plastic bag and pound with the flat side of a cleaver or the bottom of a heavy skillet. Spread on a plate; add the allspice. Dip the steak in the pepper mixture to coat evenly.

4. Heat the skillet over medium heat until hot enough to evaporate a drop of water upon contact. Add the steak and cook, covered, 5 to 6 minutes per side for rare or 7 to 8 minutes per side for medium-rare. Let stand on platter or carving board loosely covered with a piece of foil.

5. Add the broth to the hot skillet and heat to boiling over high heat. Stir in the wine and boil until reduced by half.

6. Meanwhile, halve the pieces of toast diagonally and arrange on individual plates or a large platter. Cut the steak crosswise into thin slices. Add any steak drippings to the reduced wine. Arrange the slices of steak on the toast; spoon the reduced red wine over the steak. Top with the sautéed mushrooms.

BEEF STEW *with* STEAMED VEGETABLES

Makes 4 servings

T O GIVE A FRESH VEGETABLE TASTE to this old standby, add chunks of cooked parsnips, carrots and green beans and crisp, browned cubes of potatoes just before serving. The gravy, too, is light and fresh-tasting, for it is simply a puree of all the chopped vegetables used to flavor the cooking liquid in the stew. A medley of fragrant and aromatic herbs adds the crowning glory.

<table>
<tr><td></td><td>Vegetable-oil cooking spray</td></tr>
<tr><td>1-1½</td><td>pounds of well-trimmed beef rump or top round,
   cut into 1½-inch cubes</td></tr>
<tr><td>½</td><td>cup dry red wine</td></tr>
<tr><td>½</td><td>cup diced carrot</td></tr>
<tr><td>½</td><td>cup chopped onion</td></tr>
<tr><td>½</td><td>cup chopped celery</td></tr>
<tr><td>2</td><td>garlic cloves, finely chopped</td></tr>
<tr><td>1</td><td>cup reduced-sodium or homemade beef broth (page 76)</td></tr>
<tr><td>1</td><td>cup chopped, drained canned plum tomatoes</td></tr>
<tr><td>1</td><td>sprig fresh thyme, parsley or basil, or pinch dried thyme</td></tr>
<tr><td>1</td><td>tablespoon olive oil</td></tr>
<tr><td>8</td><td>small new potatoes, halved or quartered</td></tr>
<tr><td>2</td><td>tablespoons packed fresh Italian (flat-leaf) parsley leaves
   plus tender stems</td></tr>
<tr><td>1</td><td>teaspoon fresh thyme leaves, stripped from stems,
   or ½ teaspoon dried</td></tr>
<tr><td>1</td><td>cup peeled, cubed (1-inch) parsnips</td></tr>
<tr><td>1</td><td>cup trimmed, peeled baby carrots</td></tr>
<tr><td>1</td><td>cup trimmed, cut (1-inch) fresh green beans</td></tr>
<tr><td></td><td>Salt and freshly ground black pepper to taste</td></tr>
</table>

TIPS

✴ *Choose the leaner cuts of beef whenever possible; round has about 6 grams of fat per serving, while chuck has about 15 grams.*

✴ *This recipe "sweats" the vegetables by cooking them in wine instead of butter—a handy fat-reduction technique.*

✴ *Although not as good as fresh, frozen green beans may be substituted.*

427 CALORIES PER SERVING

36 G PROTEIN

9 G FAT

47 G CARBOHYDRATE

204 MG SODIUM

76 MG CHOLESTEROL

1. Heat a large (4-to-5-quart) nonstick saucepan over medium-high heat until hot enough to evaporate a drop of water upon contact. Spray the bottom of the pan lightly with vegetable-oil cooking spray. Add the pieces of meat a few at a time; cook, turning, until browned on all sides, about 5 minutes. Transfer to a side dish.

2. Add the wine to the pan and boil 2 minutes. Add the carrot, onion, celery and 1 of the garlic cloves. Cover and cook over medium-low heat until tender, about 10 minutes.

3. Add the broth, tomatoes and thyme sprig or other herb. Return the browned meat and any juices in the dish to the saucepan. Cover and cook over low heat until the meat is fork-tender, about 1 to 1½ hours. Remove the meat to a side dish and cover with foil. Transfer the vegetables and juices to a blender or food processor and process until smooth. Return to the saucepan, add the meat, cover and keep warm.

4. Meanwhile, heat the oil in a medium (8-to-10-inch) nonstick skillet over medium-high heat until hot enough to sizzle a piece of potato. Add the potatoes, cut sides down, cover and cook over medium-low heat until almost tender, about 10 minutes. Uncover and turn heat to medium-high. Cook the potatoes, turning, until golden brown on all sides, about 5 minutes. Using a slotted spoon, transfer the potatoes to a side dish. Finely chop the parsley, thyme leaves and remaining garlic clove together, add to the potatoes and toss to coat.

5. While the potatoes are cooking, add 1 inch of water to a large (4-quart) saucepan. Set a folding steamer basket over the water. Place the parsnips, carrots and green beans in the basket. Cover and steam until tender, 8 to 10 minutes. Remove the basket from the saucepan.

6. Season the meat and pureed sauce with salt and pepper. Add the steamed vegetables; toss to coat. Add the potatoes and stir just to blend. Serve at once.

POT ROAST *with* PUREED VEGETABLE GRAVY

Makes 10 to 12 servings

190 CALORIES PER SERVING

26 G PROTEIN

6 G FAT

8 G CARBOHYDRATE

308 MG SODIUM

66 MG CHOLESTEROL

ONCE UPON A TIME, Sunday dinner in the typical American household was pot roast, served with a brown gravy made from fat drippings thickened with flour or, in the hands of more adventurous cooks, from a package of onion-soup mix. This pot roast has lots of old-fashioned flavor, without the fat or processed taste. The meat is cooked with a medley of chopped vegetables, which are then pureed to a smooth, deep-flavored sauce. Serve with broad noodles.

2 teaspoons olive oil

1 piece bottom round roast (about 3 pounds)

1 tablespoon water

1 cup chopped onion

1 cup chopped carrot

1 cup chopped celery

1 cup chopped white button mushrooms

½ cup chopped parsnip

1 garlic clove

1 can (28 ounces) Italian-style plum tomatoes with juices

1 bay leaf

½ teaspoon salt

⅛ teaspoon freshly ground black pepper

1. Preheat oven to 325 degrees F. Place 1 teaspoon of the oil in a large Dutch oven or other stovetop-to-oven pan with a tight-fitting lid. Add the roast and cook over medium-high heat, turning, until browned on all sides, about 10 minutes. Remove from the pan to a side dish.

2. Add the remaining teaspoon oil and the water to the pan; stir in the onion, carrot, celery, mushrooms and parsnip. Cover and cook over low heat, stirring occasionally, until almost tender, about 10 minutes. Add the garlic and cook over medium heat, stirring, until the vegetables begin to brown, about 5 minutes. Add the tomatoes, bay leaf, salt and pepper. Heat, breaking up the tomatoes with the side of the spoon, until boiling. Return the meat and any juices in the side dish to the pan. Spoon the vegetables over the meat. Cover and place in the oven.

3. Cook, turning the roast once or twice, until the meat is fork-tender, about 2 to 2½ hours. Remove from the oven and let stand at room temperature until cool enough to handle. Lift the meat to a side dish and let stand. Remove the bay leaf from the vegetables. Puree the vegetables and juices in a food processor or through a food mill set over a bowl. Taste the sauce and add more salt and pepper, if needed.

4. Carefully cut the meat across the grain into ¼-inch-thick slices. Serve the sliced pot roast with vegetable gravy spooned on top. (The leftovers are delicious.)

PORK STUFFED *with* DRIED APPLES & CRANBERRIES

Makes 6 to 8 servings

207 CALORIES PER SERVING

19 G PROTEIN

10 G FAT

10 G CARBOHYDRATE

227 MG SODIUM

60 MG CHOLESTEROL

PORK HAS CHANGED. Thanks to selective breeding and a lower-fat diet for the pigs, pork is about 30 percent leaner than a decade ago, and its outside blanket of fat has all but disappeared. If overcooked, today's lean pork can become dry and bland. Both moisture and flavor are added to this boneless roast with a fragrant stuffing of onion and dried fruits.

1   center or loin end boneless pork roast, well trimmed
     (about 1¾-2 pounds)
½   cup finely chopped onion
1   teaspoon olive oil
1   garlic clove, finely chopped
½   cup cooked short-grain or long-grain brown rice
¼   cup finely chopped dried apple slices
     (soak in boiling water if hard)
2   tablespoons dried cranberries or dark or golden raisins
1½   teaspoons fresh thyme leaves, stripped from the stems,
     or ¾ teaspoon dried
½   teaspoon salt
     Freshly ground black pepper

1. Preheat oven to 425 degrees F. Wipe off the surface of the meat with a damp paper towel. Using a sharp knife, cut the meat lengthwise and open it like a book. Have ready four pieces of cotton string each 12 inches long.

2. Combine the onion and oil in a large (10-to-12-inch) nonstick skillet. Cook, stirring, over medium-low heat until the onion is soft, about 5 minutes. Add the garlic; cook 1 minute. Add the rice, apples, cranberries or raisins, 1 teaspoon of the fresh thyme leaves or ½ teaspoon dried, ¼ teaspoon of the salt and a generous grinding of black pepper. Stir to blend; cook, over low heat for 3 minutes.

3. Spoon the stuffing onto the bottom half of the meat. Close the top over the stuffing. Slide the strings under the pork and tie closed. Tuck any stuffing back into the roast.

4. Place the meat in a roasting pan. Rub with the remaining ¼ teaspoon salt, ½ teaspoon fresh thyme or ¼ teaspoon dried and another grinding of pepper. Place the pan in the oven, reduce temperature to 350 degrees F and roast 30 minutes. Using a spatula, carefully turn the roast over. Roast 40 to 50 minutes longer. Let stand 15 minutes.

5. Using a long, sharp knife, cut the meat into ¼-inch-thick slices. Overlap the slices on a platter.

BARBECUED PORK
on ONION CORN BREAD

Makes 6 servings

QUICK-COOKING PORK TENDERLOINS are marinated in a zesty blend of pepper, spices and vinegar and then slowly cooked in a sweet-tart barbecue sauce until tender. Serve on Onion Corn Bread or on two slices of your favorite bread.

2	well-trimmed pork tenderloins (about 12 ounces each)
½	teaspoon crushed red pepper
¼	teaspoon ground allspice
¼	teaspoon ground cloves
¼	teaspoon salt
¼	cup cider vinegar

Barbecue Sauce

2	tablespoons vegetable oil
1	cup finely chopped onion
2	garlic cloves, finely chopped (about 1 tablespoon)
1	can (28 ounces) crushed tomatoes
2	tablespoons packed dark brown sugar
½	teaspoon salt, or more to taste
	Dash Tabasco or other hot sauce to taste
	Cider vinegar to taste
	Cayenne pepper to taste
	Onion Corn Bread (optional, page 230)

1. Wipe the surfaces of the tenderloins dry with a paper towel. Combine the red pepper, allspice, cloves and salt on a platter or rectangular glass baking dish. Add the tenderloins and rub the spices over the surfaces. Add the cider vinegar and turn to coat. Cover and refrigerate overnight, turning occasionally.

TIPS

✳ *Pork tenderloin is exemplary in both taste and healthfulness. Despite the rich promise of its name, it is nearly as low in fat as skinless chicken breast. (Pork loin and shoulder cuts contain three times as much fat.) As its name implies, the tenderloin is extremely tender.*

✳ *This is good with the Crunchy Celery Relish found in the recipe for Ground Turkey Burger (page 148).*

227 CALORIES PER SERVING

27 G PROTEIN

6 G FAT

14 G CARBOHYDRATE

545 MG SODIUM

81 MG CHOLESTEROL

2. **The following day, prepare the sauce:** Heat 1 tablespoon of the oil in a large (10-to-12-inch) skillet. Add the onion and cook, stirring, over low heat, until soft, about 10 minutes. Add the garlic; sauté 1 minute. Add the tomatoes, brown sugar and salt. Simmer, uncovered, stirring occasionally, 15 minutes.

3. Meanwhile, lift the pork tenderloins from the marinade; reserve the marinade. Heat the remaining 1 tablespoon oil in a large (4-to-5-quart) saucepan. Add the tenderloins and cook, turning, until lightly browned, about 8 minutes. Add the barbecue sauce and the reserved marinade. Cover and cook over medium-low heat, stirring and turning the meat occasionally, until the pork is tender enough to shred easily when pulled with a fork, about 2 hours. Cool slightly and shred the meat lengthwise with the grain. If necessary, cut the shreds into 2-inch lengths. Taste the sauce and add Tabasco, cider vinegar or cayenne to taste. Keep warm over low heat.

4. Meanwhile, prepare the Onion Corn Bread according to the recipe on page 230. To serve, split the corn bread squares crosswise. If desired, they can be toasted cut side up in a toaster oven or under the broiler. Reheat the pork and spoon on top.

ONION CORN BREAD

Makes 6 servings

267 CALORIES PER SERVING

6 G PROTEIN

10 G FAT

37 G CARBOHYDRATE

373 MG SODIUM

2 MG CHOLESTEROL

CUT THE FAT AND CALORIES IN TRADITIONAL CORN BREAD by preparing it with low-fat milk, vegetable oil and egg white instead of whole milk, bacon drippings and a whole egg.

Vegetable-oil cooking spray
2 tablespoons vegetable oil
⅓ cup chopped onion
1 cup all-purpose flour
1 cup yellow cornmeal
1 tablespoon baking powder
½ teaspoon salt
¼ teaspoon freshly ground black pepper
1 cup low-fat milk
1 egg white

1. Preheat oven to 400 degrees F. Spray an 8-inch square pan with cooking spray.

2. Heat the oil in a small skillet over medium-low heat. Add the onion and cook, stirring, until golden, about 5 minutes. Set aside.

3. In a large bowl, combine the flour, cornmeal, baking powder, salt and pepper. In a measuring cup, whisk the milk, egg white and cooked onion mixture together until blended. Add to the dry ingredients all at once. Stir just to blend; do not overmix.

4. Spread in the prepared pan. Bake until the sides begin to pull away from the pan, about 20 minutes. Cool on a rack before loosening the sides and turning out of the pan.

5. Divide into 6 squares.

SEAFOOD CAKES *with* CRUNCHY SAUCE

Makes 4 servings

FISH CAKES USED TO CONJURE UP IMAGES of blandness. This revision of a long-lived classic should do wonders to dispel that view. These cream-colored seafood-rice cakes are lightened with specks of pale green leek, red pepper and fresh basil. For the standard tartar sauce, substitute a homemade "sauce" of minced fresh vegetables in a light mayonnaise base. Use absolutely any cooked fish or shellfish—or a mixture of the two.

2   cups warm, moist, cooked long-grain white or brown rice
1   cup cooked, flaked, skinless, boneless fish
       (cod, salmon, trout, snapper or any other fish;
       or crab, minced shrimp, lobster; or any combination)
2   teaspoons olive oil
½   cup finely chopped white and pale green part
       of a well-rinsed small leek
1   tablespoon water
2   tablespoons finely chopped red bell pepper
1   garlic clove, crushed through a press
2   tablespoons chopped fresh basil or fresh Italian
       (flat-leaf) parsley
1   teaspoon grated lemon zest
2   egg whites
1   teaspoon butter
4   lemon wedges
    Crunchy Sauce (page 233)

Crunchy Sauce (page 233)

TIPS

❋ *One cup flaked fish is equal to about 8 ounces raw, but the sensible approach is to grill, broil or bake an extra fillet or steak to have on hand for these seafood cakes. Use fresh cooked rice (either white, brown or a combination of the two) that is still warm, or heat leftover rice by sprinkling it with 1 tablespoon water and reheating it, covered, in the microwave for about 2 minutes.*

❋ *Do not use converted or parboiled rice because it is not sticky enough to hold the cakes together.*

230 CALORIES PER SERVING

15 G PROTEIN

4 G FAT

32 G CARBOHYDRATE

74 MG SODIUM

27 MG CHOLESTEROL

1. In a large bowl, combine the rice and the fish and/or seafood. Combine 1 teaspoon of the olive oil and the leek in a large (10-to-12-inch) nonstick skillet; sprinkle with the water and cook, covered, over medium-low heat until tender, about 5 minutes; do not brown.

2. Add the red bell pepper and garlic and sauté 2 minutes. Remove from the heat; add this mixture along with the basil or parsley and lemon zest to the rice mixture. Whisk the egg whites in a small bowl until frothy; add them to the rice mixture; stir until blended.

3. Dampen your hands with cold water and measure out ⅓ cupfuls of the seafood-rice mixture; shape into 8 cakes approximately 3 inches across and ½ inch thick. Place on a plate and let stand, uncovered, at least 15 minutes at room temperature or up to 1 hour refrigerated, before cooking.

4. Wipe out the skillet. Heat the remaining 1 teaspoon olive oil and the butter in the skillet until sizzling. Add the cakes and cook until well browned, 5 to 6 minutes per side.

5. Serve 2 cakes per person, along with a lemon wedge and Crunchy Sauce.

CRUNCHY SAUCE

Makes about 1 cup or enough for 8 servings

CRUNCHY SAUCE IS A FRESH-TASTING SUBSTITUTE for tartar sauce. Reduced-calorie mayonnaise has half the fat and calories of regular because it is made with added water, which "stretches" it further, saving fat.

½ cup reduced-calorie mayonnaise, strained yogurt (page 201) or a combination of half yogurt and half reduced-calorie mayonnaise

1 tablespoon peeled, seeded, minced cucumber

1 tablespoon minced green bell pepper

1 tablespoon minced celery

1 tablespoon cider vinegar

1 tablespoon chopped fresh basil or fresh Italian (flat-leaf) parsley

1 tablespoon chopped fresh dill

½ teaspoon grated lemon zest

½ teaspoon grated orange zest

42 CALORIES PER SERVING

0 G PROTEIN

4 G FAT

1 G CARBOHYDRATE

1 MG SODIUM

5 MG CHOLESTEROL

In a bowl, combine the mayonnaise or yogurt, cucumber, green bell pepper, celery, vinegar, basil or parsley, dill and lemon and orange zests. Stir to blend. Serve at once or cover and refrigerate until ready to serve.

OVEN-FRIED FISH FILLETS

Makes 4 servings

IF YOU LIKE YOUR FISH covered with a crisp breading—but want to avoid the fat and calories that come with deep-fat frying—dip the fillets in a lightly beaten egg white instead of a whole egg, dredge them in seasoned crumbs and bake them in a hot oven.

2	teaspoons olive oil
½	cup all-purpose flour
½	teaspoon salt
	Freshly ground black pepper
1	egg white
1	cup fine, dry bread crumbs
1	teaspoon grated lemon zest
1	teaspoon fresh thyme leaves, stripped from the stems, or ½ teaspoon dried
1	pound fish fillets (cod, blackfish, salmon, catfish or sole), cut into 4 portions
	Lemon wedges and whole thyme sprigs (optional garnish)

1. Preheat oven to 450 degrees F. Brush a nonstick baking sheet lightly with a thin film of the olive oil.

2. Place the flour, salt and pepper on a large sheet of wax paper. Whisk the egg white in a shallow soup bowl or pie plate until frothy. Combine the crumbs, lemon zest and thyme on a second sheet of wax paper.

3. Turn the fish portions in the flour mixture to coat; shake off excess. Dip in the egg to coat. Turn in the bread crumbs, using your fingertips to press the crumbs onto the fish. Place on the prepared baking sheet.

4. Bake on an oven rack placed in lowest position until golden on the bottom, about 4 minutes. Remove the baking sheet from the oven and, using a wide spatula, carefully turn the fillets over. Bake until golden and crisp, 3 to 4 minutes.

5. Serve garnished with lemon wedges and thyme sprigs, if desired.

BAKED SCALLOPS *with* CIDER SAUCE

Makes 4 servings

163 CALORIES PER SERVING

20 G PROTEIN

3 G FAT

14 G CARBOHYDRATE

210 MG SODIUM

42 MG CHOLESTEROL

IN ITS ORIGINAL FORM, this favorite recipe used one whole slice of bacon per person and butter to emulsify the cider sauce. Here, a single slice of bacon is cut into thin slivers and divided over the scallops. The cider sauce is thickened with a small amount of cornstarch.

12	large sea scallops (about 1-1¼ pounds)
	Oil for coating the pan
1	strip lean bacon, cut in ⅛-inch crosswise slivers
1	teaspoon unsalted butter
1	Golden Delicious apple, cored and cut into 16 thin wedges
¼	teaspoon sugar
⅔	cup apple cider or apple juice
1¼	teaspoons cornstarch
1	tablespoon fresh lemon juice
	Salt
	Freshly ground black pepper
3	large basil leaves, stacked, rolled from top to bottom and sliced in thin rounds to create long strips

1. Preheat oven to 425 degrees F.

2. Arrange the scallops on a lightly oiled baking dish. Divide the bacon slivers into 12 equal portions and place each one on top of each scallop. Bake until the scallops are just cooked through, 8 to 10 minutes, depending on the size and thickness of the scallops.

3. While the scallops are cooking, melt the butter in a large (10-inch) nonstick skillet. Add the apple slices and sugar and cook over medium heat, turning occasionally, until the apples turn golden, about 5 minutes.

4. Stir the cider or apple juice and the cornstarch together until well blended and add this mixture and the lemon juice to the apples. Increase the heat and stir constantly until the sauce thickens. Season with salt and pepper.

5. Arrange 3 bacon-topped scallops and 4 apple slices on each of four dinner plates. Spoon the sauce over the scallops and top with the basil strips.

OVEN-ROASTED FISH STEAKS

Makes 4 servings

✳ This recipe can be varied in any number of ways. Use salmon, swordfish, halibut, mako shark, tilefish, codfish or any firm-fleshed, thick steaks.

✳ Fish is cooked through when the flesh at the thickest part has turned from translucent to opaque. Make a slit with the point of a small knife to test for doneness.

236 CALORIES PER SERVING

28 G PROTEIN

8 G FAT

12 G CARBOHYDRATE

126 MG SODIUM

54 MG CHOLESTEROL

FISH BAKED AT A HOT TEMPERATURE for a short period of time is convenient and delicious. A ½-to-1-inch-thick fish steak will bake in a hot oven in 10 to 15 minutes.

2   large Spanish onions, halved lengthwise,
      cut into thin half circles (about 3½ cups)
1   red bell pepper, halved, seeds, stem and ribs removed,
      cut into thin lengthwise strips
1   strip (2-x-½-inch) orange zest, cut into very thin
      lengthwise strips
1   teaspoon fresh thyme or rosemary leaves,
      stripped from the stems, or ½ teaspoon dried thyme
2   teaspoons olive oil
4   fish steaks, each ½-1 inch thick
      Salt
      Freshly ground black pepper
      Sprigs of thyme or rosemary for garnish

1. Preheat oven to 400 degrees F. Combine the onions, red pepper, orange zest and thyme or rosemary in a large baking pan; add the olive oil; stir to blend.

2. Roast the vegetables, stirring every 10 minutes, until golden, about 25 minutes. Remove the pan from the oven; turn the oven to 450 degrees F. Push the vegetables to the sides and arrange the fish steaks in the pan. Spoon some of the vegetables over the tops of the fish steaks. Sprinkle lightly with salt and add a grinding of black pepper.

3. Bake the fish 10 minutes. Remove the pan from the oven and, using the tip of a small knife, check the fish for doneness. The fish is cooked when its flesh turns from translucent to opaque. If necessary, continue cooking, 1 to 2 minutes more at a time, until the fish is done.

4. Serve the fish steaks topped with the vegetables. Garnish the platter with sprigs of thyme or rosemary.

Chapter 8

DESSERTS

DESSERTS

WHAT ARE THESE?" asked my husband, as he innocently munched away on a moist, chocolate-flavored square. I didn't let on that I had hoped they would be a breakthrough in my quest for the perfect reduced-fat brownie. In this version—and there were several—I had used raspberry jam and cocoa along with vegetable oil and egg whites instead of whole eggs. The squares looked brown and flat, just like brownies should. But the rich, chewy texture and overwhelmingly chocolaty taste were missing. If my husband didn't recognize it as a brownie, I obviously hadn't succeeded.

Reducing fat in baked desserts without sacrificing flavor and texture has always been a challenge. Having worked as a professional baker, I never underestimate the power of real butter. In some desserts, nothing else tastes as good. Many cakes, tarts, puddings, soufflés, iced desserts and sweet sauces, however, stand up well to a little pinching and tucking in their fat contents. Nibbling on my "brownie," I re-

solved not to fool with recipes that could not be streamlined without disappointing and, instead, set about trying to lighten those that I suspected could accept some straightforward substitutions.

I soon discovered that soufflés can rise to the same height with half as many yolks as traditionally called for, and that cocoa powder, which is low in fat, can deliver as rich a chocolate hit as high-fat baking chocolate. In cheesecake, light cream cheese imparts the same texture and fullness as regular, but with half the fat.

It is easy to produce a crumbly crust for pies and tarts with vegetable oil instead of butter or shortening, which contain saturated fat. In many cakes, butter is not necessary; vegetable oil can yield as moist and light a crumb.

STILL, NO DESSERT WORTH ITS NAME is really improved by simply taking ingredients away. Sweet, fruity or other richly flavored additions are essential. Strong coffee can fortify low-fat chocolate cake; the zing of orange or lemon zest livens light custards; the nutlike taste of whole-wheat flour enriches pastry without butter, and a generous hand with ginger, cinnamon and other spices in cakes made with oil keeps the tastebuds alert and satisfied.

Perhaps the best antidote to missing fat is sweetness itself, which, when used in a considered fashion, can satisfy and divert the palate, whether it is a crumb topping on a coffee cake, cooked fruit on an upside-down cake or caramelized sugar on crème caramel.

As for my brownies, I still serve them on occasion—unadulterated, of course. In between, this collection of favorites reminds me that it is quite possible to enjoy a little sweetness without a lot of guilt.

CHOCOLATE PUDDING

Makes 4 servings

THE FLAVOR OF THIS RICH CHOCOLATE PUDDING is so much better than packaged that you will never go back. It is also one of the easiest desserts to make from scratch. This family classic was customarily made with whole milk and solid baking chocolate. Now I use cocoa powder and low-fat milk.

⅓ cup unsweetened cocoa powder
½ cup sugar
2 tablespoons plus 2 teaspoons cornstarch
2 cups low-fat milk
1 teaspoon vanilla extract

1. In a medium (3-quart) saucepan, stir the cocoa, sugar and cornstarch together until evenly blended.

2. Heat over medium-low heat and gradually stir in the milk. Cook, stirring constantly, until the mixture is boiling, thick and smooth. Cool 5 minutes; stir in the vanilla.

3. Pour into four individual ½-cup custard cups. Serve warm or at room temperature.

TIP

✴ *Unsweetened cocoa powder has only 115 calories and 4 grams of fat in ⅓ cup, compared with 139 calories and 14 grams of fat in 1 ounce of unsweetened baking chocolate.*

182 CALORIES PER SERVING

6 G PROTEIN

2 G FAT

39 G CARBOHYDRATE

67 MG SODIUM

5 MG CHOLESTEROL

ORANGE CRÈME CARAMEL

Makes 6 servings

161 CALORIES PER SERVING

5 G PROTEIN

3 G FAT

29 G CARBOHYDRATE

64 MG SODIUM

110 MG CHOLESTEROL

CRÈME CARAMEL, baked custard topped with a syrup made from caramelized sugar, is a beloved dessert. Low-fat or skim milk substitutes nicely for regular milk or cream, and egg whites replace some of the yolks.

3   strips orange zest, each ½ x 3 inches
    (removed with a vegetable peeler)

Caramelized Sugar

½   cup sugar
3   tablespoons water

Custard

2   cups low-fat milk
1   tablespoon coarsely chopped orange zest
1   cinnamon stick
3   whole cloves
2   large eggs
1   egg yolk
¼   cup sugar
1   teaspoon vanilla extract

1. Select six 4-to-6-ounce custard cups or soufflé dishes. Stack the strips of orange zest and cut lengthwise into very thin julienne strips. Divide them evenly among the custard cups.

2. **Making the caramelized sugar:** Bring the ½ cup sugar and the water to a boil over medium heat in a small skillet, stirring, until the sugar is completely dissolved. Increase the heat to high and boil, without stirring, until the syrup turns golden, about 8 minutes. Immediately pour a little of the caramelized sugar into each custard cup over the orange zest, dividing it evenly; set aside.

3. **Making the custard:** Combine the milk, orange zest, cinnamon and whole cloves in a small saucepan and heat, over low heat, until small bubbles appear around the edges of the milk. Remove from heat and let stand, covered, 20 minutes. Strain and discard the solids. Reserve the flavored milk.

4. Preheat oven to 325 degrees F. Beat the whole eggs, egg yolk, ¼ cup sugar and vanilla in a bowl until blended. Slowly whisk in the warm milk; do not overbeat, or the milk will become too frothy. Pour the custard into the prepared custard cups, dividing it evenly.

5. Place the custard cups on a rack in a large baking pan and set in the oven. Carefully pour enough very hot water into the baking pan to come halfway up the sides of the custard cups. Bake just until the edges are set and the center just barely quivers when a cup is moved, about 55 minutes.

6. Let the custards cool in the hot water for 1 hour. Loosen the edges with the tip of a knife. Place a dessert plate over each custard cup and quickly invert each custard onto its plate.

MAPLE RICE PUDDING

Makes 4 servings

SATISFYING BOTH THE BUSY and the health-conscious rice pudding lover, this dessert has also been known to convert those who don't usually like rice puddings of any kind. The calories and fat have been reduced by using low-fat or skim milk and by omitting the eggs. Maple syrup adds gentle sweetness.

Pudding

1	quart skim or low-fat milk
2	cups cooked long-grain white rice (do not use parboiled or converted rice)
⅓	cup pure maple syrup
1	teaspoon grated orange zest
1	teaspoon vanilla extract

Maple-Toasted Walnuts

⅓	cup walnut pieces
2	tablespoons pure maple syrup

1. **Making the rice pudding:** Combine the milk and rice in a large, wide saucepan. Cook, stirring, over medium-low heat until the mixture boils and thickens, about 25 minutes. Stir in the maple syrup and cook 10 minutes more.

2. Add the orange zest and vanilla. Pour into four 8-ounce dessert bowls or custard cups; cool at room temperature.

3. **Meanwhile, make the walnuts:** Heat the walnuts in a small, heavy skillet over low heat, stirring, until fragrant, about 3 minutes. Drizzle the maple syrup over the walnuts and cook, over medium heat, stirring, until the syrup boils and coats the walnuts, about 2 minutes. Sprinkle on the puddings, dividing them evenly.

TIP

❋ *The Maple-Toasted Walnuts are so sweetly crunchy that you'll be hard put not to eat them all out of hand.*

384 CALORIES PER SERVING

14 G PROTEIN

7 G FAT

69 G CARBOHYDRATE

165 MG SODIUM

4 MG CHOLESTEROL

LEMON SOUFFLÉS
with APRICOT JAM

Makes 6 servings

TIP

❋ *Eggs whip best at room temperature or warmer.*

119 CALORIES PER SERVING

4 G PROTEIN

3 G FAT

20 G CARBOHYDRATE

58 MG SODIUM

107 MG CHOLESTEROL

SOUFFLÉS ARE THE ULTIMATE IN ELEGANT DESSERTS—and they are surprisingly easy to make. Savvy cooks, with an eye on fat intake, have been successfully reformulating traditional soufflé recipes so that they use half the number of yolks. These tangy lemon soufflés are partially sweetened with a spoonful of reduced-sugar apricot preserves.

Vegetable-oil cooking spray
Sugar for dusting the soufflé dishes
6 tablespoons reduced-sugar apricot preserves
3 large egg yolks
4 large egg whites
6 tablespoons sugar
3 tablespoons fresh lemon juice
2 teaspoons grated lemon zest
¼ teaspoon almond extract
Confectioners' sugar

1. Preheat oven to 425 degrees F. Spray the insides of six 6-ounce soufflé dishes or custard cups with vegetable-oil cooking spray; sprinkle the bottoms and sides lightly with the sugar. Place 1 tablespoon of the apricot preserves in the bottom of each prepared soufflé dish and set aside.

2. Whisk the egg yolks and 1 of the egg whites in a medium bowl just until blended. Add the sugar and whisk until the mixture is pale yellow. Gradually whisk in the lemon juice, lemon zest and almond extract.

3. Beat the remaining 3 egg whites with an electric mixer until soft peaks form. Fold the whites into the yolks in two additions. Spoon the batter into the prepared soufflé dishes, filling the dishes almost to the tops.

4. Bake until the soufflés are puffed and golden, 10 to 12 minutes. Sift a little confectioners' sugar over each one and serve at once.

VERY CHOCOLATE ICE MILK

Makes about 3 cups or 6 servings

COCOA IS A TASTY AND HEALTHFUL ALTERNATIVE to chocolate bars or squares of chocolate. This chocolate ice milk is intense but not overwhelming. Its taste reminds me a little of the frozen chocolate on a stick called fudgesicles that we ate as kids.

⅓   cup unsweetened cocoa powder
⅓   cup sugar
2   cups low-fat milk
½   teaspoon vanilla extract

1. In a small saucepan, stir the cocoa and sugar until blended. Stir in the milk and cook, stirring, over medium-low heat until the sugar and cocoa dissolve, about 5 minutes. Do not boil.

2. If using an ice-cream maker, refrigerate the mixture until chilled and then freeze according to the manufacturer's directions. Or, if preferred, pour the mixture into a 9- or 10-inch metal cake pan and place in the freezer compartment of the refrigerator. Freeze, stirring the firm outside edges into the soft center every 30 to 45 minutes, until the mixture is frozen solid. Transfer to the bowl of a food processor. Add the vanilla and process until smooth. Pack into a plastic freezer container and freeze at least 2 hours or overnight before serving.

PEACH ICE MILK

Makes about 3 cups or 6 servings

T HE FLAVOR OF THIS FROZEN PUREED MIXTURE of sliced peaches, low-fat milk and sugar depends entirely on the ripeness and flavor of the peaches. For optimal flavor, choose fresh, seasonal fruit. Good-quality unsweetened frozen fruit, thawed, can also be used. I have made this same dessert with nectarines, strawberries and apricots—let the market and your own taste be the judge.

2 cups peeled, sliced peaches, strawberries or apricots
1 cup low-fat milk
3 tablespoons sugar
1 teaspoon fresh lime juice, or to taste
½ teaspoon vanilla extract (optional)

Combine the fruit, milk, sugar, lime juice and vanilla, if using, in the bowl of a food processor. Process until very smooth. Taste and add more lime juice, if desired. Freeze in an ice-cream maker, following the manufacturer's instructions. Or, pour the mixture into a 9- or 10-inch metal cake pan and place in the freezer compartment of the refrigerator. Freeze, stirring the firm outside edges into the soft center every 30 to 45 minutes, until the mixture is frozen solid. Spoon into the food processor and process until smooth. Pack into a plastic freezer container and freeze at least 2 hours or overnight before serving.

TIPS

✳ *Taste the mixture, and if the fruit seems lackluster, add about ½ teaspoon lime juice, or more as needed, to add acid and heighten the flavor.*

✳ *Mangoes and peaches are another good combination.*

64 CALORIES PER SERVING

2 G PROTEIN

0.5 G FAT

14 G CARBOHYDRATE

21 MG SODIUM

2 MG CHOLESTEROL

VERY MOCHA ICE MILK

Makes about 3 cups or 6 servings

A VARIATION ON VERY CHOCOLATE ICE MILK, this one goes over well with grown-ups. Strong espresso coffee intensifies the rich flavor.

⅓ cup unsweetened cocoa powder
⅓ cup sugar, plus more to taste
1½ cups low-fat milk
½ cup brewed espresso coffee
½ teaspoon vanilla extract

78 CALORIES PER SERVING

3 G PROTEIN

1 G FAT

16 G CARBOHYDRATE

35 MG SODIUM

3 MG CHOLESTEROL

1. In a small saucepan, stir the cocoa and ⅓ cup sugar until blended. Stir in the milk and espresso and cook, stirring, over medium-low heat until the sugar and cocoa dissolve. Taste and add 1 tablespoon more sugar, if desired. Continue to cook, stirring, over medium-low heat for about 5 minutes. Do not boil.

2. If using an ice-cream maker, refrigerate the mixture until chilled and then freeze according to the manufacturer's directions. Or, if preferred, pour the mixture into a 9- or 10-inch metal cake pan and place in the freezer compartment of the refrigerator. Freeze, stirring the firm outside edges into the soft center every 30 to 45 minutes, until the mixture is frozen solid. Transfer to the bowl of a food processor. Add the vanilla and process until smooth. Pack into a plastic freezer container and freeze at least 2 hours or overnight before serving.

DEEP MOCHA SAUCE

Makes about 1 cup

36 CALORIES PER TABLESPOON

0 G PROTEIN

0.3 G FAT

9 G CARBOHYDRATE

2 MG SODIUM

0 MG CHOLESTEROL

AN EASY, SOPHISTICATED TAKE-OFF on Deep Chocolate Sauce, with espresso supplying its intense, rich kick.

⅓   cup unsweetened cocoa powder
⅔   cup sugar
¾   cup brewed espresso coffee
1   teaspoon vanilla extract

1. Stir the cocoa and sugar in a medium saucepan until blended. Gradually stir in the coffee until blended and smooth. Heat to boiling, stirring constantly.

2. Boil, adjusting the heat to prevent the sauce from boiling over, 5 minutes. Transfer to a bowl and cool. Stir in the vanilla.

DEEP CHOCOLATE SAUCE

Makes about 1 cup

EVERYONE LOVES CHOCOLATE—especially chocolate sauce. For years, my favorite sauce was a boiled mixture of chocolate, heavy cream and sugar. The following chocolate sauce, made without the cream, is full-flavored but not full of fat, and very, very good.

⅓ cup unsweetened cocoa powder
⅔ cup sugar
¾ cup water
1 teaspoon vanilla extract

1. Stir the cocoa and sugar in a medium saucepan until blended. Gradually stir in the water until blended and smooth. Heat to boiling, stirring constantly.

2. Boil, stirring frequently, adjusting the heat to prevent the sauce from boiling over, 5 minutes. Transfer to a bowl and cool. Stir in the vanilla.

TIP

✳ *This sauce keeps well in the refrigerator, so make up an extra batch and keep it on hand for a quick chocolate fix—over frozen yogurt, of course.*

35 SERVINGS PER TABLESPOON

0 G PROTEIN

0.3 G FAT

9 G CARBOHYDRATE

2 MG SODIUM

0 MG CHOLESTEROL

RASPBERRY &
STRAWBERRY SAUCE

Makes about 1⅔ cups

6 CALORIES PER TABLESPOON

0 G PROTEIN

0 G FAT

2 G CARBOHYDRATE

2 MG SODIUM

0 MG CHOLESTEROL

TAKE ADVANTAGE OF THE CONCENTRATED FLAVOR of sugar-free preserves and jelly to sweeten sauces and desserts.

1   cup fresh or frozen, thawed unsweetened raspberries

1   cup sliced fresh or frozen, thawed unsweetened strawberries

⅓   cup water

2   tablespoons sugar-free raspberry or strawberry preserves

     or 1 tablespoon sugar, or to taste

1   teaspoon fresh lime juice, or to taste

Combine the raspberries, strawberries, water, preserves or sugar and lime juice in the bowl of a food processor. Puree until smooth. Press through a strainer to remove the seeds. Taste and add more sugar or lime juice, if needed.

VANILLA CUSTARD SAUCE

Makes 1½ cups

THE RICHNESS OF THIS SAUCE, which might otherwise have disappeared when the eggs in the usual preparation were reduced, has been recovered by steeping a whole vanilla bean in the milk. Vanilla has a unique ability to contribute depth and flavor to a dish.

2   cups low-fat milk
½   vanilla bean (about 2½ inches)
¼   cup sugar
1   tablespoon cornstarch
1   large egg

1. In a small saucepan, combine the milk and vanilla bean. Heat over medium-low heat until small bubbles appear around the edges of the milk. Remove from the heat, cover and let stand for 30 minutes. Lift the vanilla bean from the milk; split it along one side and, using the tip of a small spoon, scrape the small beans and sticky paste from the pod into the milk. Discard the pod.

2. Stir the sugar and cornstarch in a clean saucepan until blended. Gradually add the milk until blended. Cook, stirring, over medium heat until the mixture is thickened; remove from the heat.

3. Whisk the egg in a small bowl until frothy. Gradually whisk in a few spoonfuls of the hot milk mixture. Whisk the egg mixture back into the saucepan. Cook, stirring, over low heat until the mixture is just a little thicker. Do not boil. Cool, stirring occasionally.

4. Cover and chill before using.

TIP

❋ *For more on vanilla beans, see page 258.*

❋ *This is excellent served with Lemon Sponge Cake (page 274), Winter Fruit Tart (page 258), a poached pear or over sliced strawberries.*

20 CALORIES PER TABLESPOON
1 G PROTEIN
0.4 G FAT
3 G CARBOHYDRATE
13 MG SODIUM
10 MG CHOLESTEROL

WINTER FRUIT TART

Makes 6 servings

❋ *For a tender crust, always roll it out between two sheets of wax paper. The paper allows you to roll the crust thin without using extra flour, which will make it dry and tough.*

❋ *Calimyrna figs are available dried and loosely packed in bags in the dried-fruit section of supermarkets. They make a delicious snack. The word is a combination of California, where they are grown, and Smyrna, Turkey, where they are purported to have been originally cultivated.*

❋ *The flavor coaxed from a vanilla bean is full and round. They are available in the spice section in most supermarkets, but if you don't have a whole bean, you can stir 1 teaspoon vanilla extract into the figs after they are partially cooled.*

MAKE THIS TART CRUST with a monounsaturated oil, such as canola or light olive oil, which is nearly flavorless. It will be crisp and flaky rather than cookielike. This tart is lovely with Vanilla Custard Sauce (page 257).

Filling

1	8-ounce package dried Calimyrna figs, stems trimmed, quartered (about 1½ cups)
½	cup golden raisins
½	cup dried apple chunks
1	2-inch piece vanilla bean, split
2	cups unsweetened apple juice (or for a less sweet filling, half apple juice and half water)

Crust

1	cup all-purpose flour
¼	cup whole-wheat flour
1	teaspoon ground cinnamon
½	teaspoon salt
¼	cup mild-flavored vegetable oil
3	tablespoons low-fat milk, or more as needed

2	large ripe Bosc pears, peeled, cored and quartered, cut into ½-inch wedges
2	tablespoons sliced natural (unblanched) almonds

1. **Making the filling:** Combine the figs, raisins, dried apples, vanilla bean and apple juice in a medium saucepan. Heat to boiling. Reduce the heat to low and cook, covered, until the fruit is tender, about 25 minutes. Uncover, increase the heat and boil until the liquid is evaporated and the fruit is dry, about 2 minutes, depending on the amount of liquid. Transfer to a platter and cool in the refrigerator. Remove the vanilla bean before using the filling.

2. **Meanwhile, make the crust:** Combine the flours, cinnamon and salt in a bowl; gradually add the oil while stirring quickly with a fork until the mixture is crumbly. Drizzle in the milk and toss with a fork until the dough forms. Gather into a ball and roll the crust between two sheets of wax paper into a 10-inch circle. Fit the dough into the bottom and up the sides of a 9-inch loose-bottomed tart pan. Use any excess dough to reinforce the sides of the shell to make a rigid edge.

3. Preheat oven to 400 degrees F. Spread the cooled dried-fruit filling in the tart shell. Arrange the pears, on their sides, in a sunburst pattern, pressing them into the filling. Sprinkle with the almonds.

4. Bake in the preheated oven 15 minutes. Reduce the heat to 350 degrees F and bake 30 minutes more, or until the crust is browned.

5. Cool on a rack. Carefully remove the outside rim of the tart pan.

408 CALORIES PER SERVING
5 G PROTEIN
12 G FAT
76 G CARBOHYDRATE
197 MG SODIUM
0 MG CHOLESTEROL

STRAWBERRY TART

Makes 6 to 8 servings

TAKE ADVANTAGE OF STRAWBERRIES' natural sweetness and intense flavor by using the freshest, juiciest berries you can find.

Crust

1¼	cups all-purpose flour
2	tablespoons sugar
1	teaspoon grated lemon zest
	Pinch of salt
¼	cup vegetable oil
2-3	tablespoons ice water

Strawberry Filling

2	pints ripe strawberries, rinsed and hulled
½	cup sugar
3	tablespoons cornstarch
½	cup water
1	tablespoon fresh lemon juice

Confectioners' sugar

1. **Making the crust:** Stir the flour, sugar, zest and salt together in a large bowl. Drizzle with the vegetable oil while stirring the mixture with a fork until it forms coarse crumbs. Then stir in the ice water, 1 tablespoon at a time, until the mixture begins to pull away from the sides of the bowl. Gather into a ball and flatten into a round disk. Roll out at once or wrap in foil and refrigerate up to 2 hours.

2. Preheat oven to 400 degrees F. Roll the dough between two sheets of wax paper until just large enough to fit a 9-inch loose-bottomed tart pan. (Dampen the countertop to keep the paper from slipping.) Transfer to the tart pan. The dough will be slightly crumbly; mend any tears by pressing it together with your fingertips. Press the dough along the bottom and up the sides of the pan. Use any extra dough to reinforce the sides of the tart. Line the tart with a clean sheet of wax paper and weight it with dried beans or raw rice. Bake 10 minutes. Remove the wax paper and weights and bake until the crust is golden, about 10 minutes. Cool on a wire rack. Carefully remove the outside rim of the tart pan and slide the bottom of the pan onto a serving platter.

3. **Making the filling:** Reserve 1 pint of the most perfect berries for the top of the tart; cut in half and set aside. Cut the remaining berries into thin slices.

4. In a medium (3-quart) saucepan, combine the sugar and the cornstarch; stir until thoroughly blended. Gradually stir in the water until the mixture is smooth; add half of the thinly sliced strawberries. Cook, stirring constantly and mashing the berries with the back of a spoon, until the mixture is boiling, thick and shiny. Remove from the heat and gently stir in the reserved thinly sliced berries and the lemon juice.

5. About 1 hour before serving, spoon the strawberry filling into the tart shell. Gently smooth the top. Refrigerate until set. Arrange the halved, perfect berries evenly, cut side down, on top of the filling in tight concentric circles. Sprinkle lightly with the confectioners' sugar.

297 CALORIES PER SERVING

3 G PROTEIN

10 G FAT

51 G CARBOHYDRATE

47 MG SODIUM

0 MG CHOLESTEROL

FRUIT SALAD *with* SPICED SYRUP

Makes 6 servings

119 CALORIES PER SERVING

1 G PROTEIN

1 G FAT

31 G CARBOHYDRATE

9 MG SODIUM

0 MG CHOLESTEROL

THIS FRUIT SALAD, chilled in a syrup spiced with a bay leaf and cloves, is exquisite, especially if served with a scoop of lime sherbet.

Syrup

1   cup water

⅓   cup sugar

5   whole cloves

1   tablespoon dried cherries, cranberries, currants or raisins

1   cinnamon stick

1   bay leaf

1   strip orange zest, 1½-×-2½-inch, cut in thin slivers

Fruit

1   mango, peeled, pitted and cut in ¾-inch cubes

2   cups cantaloupe, seeded, peeled and cut in ¾-inch cubes

1   cup Asian pear, Bosc pear or apple, peeled, cored and cut in ¾-inch cubes

2   kiwis, peeled and cut into ⅓-inch cubes

1   lime, peeled, white pith removed, sectioned

1. **Making the syrup:** In a small (2-quart) saucepan, stir together the water, sugar, cloves, dried fruit, cinnamon stick, bay leaf and orange zest. Cook, stirring occasionally, over medium-low heat for 20 minutes. Cool to room temperature.

2. **Making the fruit:** Combine the mango, cantaloupe, pear or apple, kiwis and lime in a bowl. Set aside.

3. Add the cooled syrup to the fruit; stir to blend. Refrigerate, covered, until very cold. Remove the cloves, cinnamon stick, bay leaf and orange zest before serving.

ORANGE CHEESECAKE & STRAWBERRIES

Makes 12 servings

SERVE THE CHEESECAKE PLAIN, with a fruit sauce spooned over it, or garnish it with whole berries or slices of fruit.

Crust
1 cup finely crushed vanilla wafers
½ teaspoon ground cinnamon
1 tablespoon egg white
Vegetable-oil cooking spray

Cheesecake
1 container (16 ounces) low-fat cottage cheese
1 package (8 ounces) light cream cheese (neufchâtel), at room temperature
⅓ cup sugar
1 tablespoon all-purpose flour
2 tablespoons orange juice
1½ teaspoons grated orange zest
1 teaspoon vanilla extract
1 large navel orange, sectioned, membranes removed
1 pint ripe strawberries, sliced thinly

1. **Making the crust:** Preheat oven to 350 degrees F. Combine the vanilla wafers and cinnamon in a bowl. In a separate bowl, whisk the egg white until foamy and blend it into the crumbs with a fork.

2. Spray a 9-inch springform pan with vegetable-oil cooking spray. Press the crumbs in an even layer in the bottom of the prepared pan. Bake 10 minutes. Cool. Reduce the oven temperature to 300 degrees F.

3. **Making the cheesecake:** In the bowl of a food processor, combine the cottage cheese, cream cheese, sugar, flour, orange juice, orange zest and vanilla extract until very smooth. Spoon into the prepared crust and smooth the top with a rubber spatula.

4. Bake until set in the center, about 35 to 40 minutes. Cool in the pan. Refrigerate until cold. Loosen the sides of the cake with a small spatula and remove the pan rim.

5. Combine the orange sections and strawberries. Cut the cheesecake into thin wedges and spoon some fruit on each serving.

137 CALORIES PER SERVING

8 G PROTEIN

5 G FAT

17 G CARBOHYDRATE

281 MG SODIUM

12 MG CHOLESTEROL

WALNUT CRUMB COFFEE CAKE

Makes 8 servings

A TENDER, MOIST, QUICK-TO-ASSEMBLE COFFEE CAKE, guaranteed to become a family favorite. Instead of butter, margarine or hydrogenated shortening, I use vegetable oil.

Topping

½	cup chopped walnuts
½	cup brown sugar
2	teaspoons ground cinnamon
2	tablespoons vegetable oil

Cake

1¾	cups all-purpose flour
2	teaspoons baking powder
1	teaspoon baking soda
1	teaspoon ground cinnamon
½	teaspoon salt
1	cup low-fat plain yogurt
⅓	cup vegetable oil
⅓	cup honey
1	large egg
1	teaspoon vanilla extract

1. Preheat oven to 350 degrees F. Spray a 9-inch cake pan with vegetable-oil cooking spray; sprinkle with flour and shake out excess.

TIP

✳ *Although neither margarine nor shortening has cholesterol, they do contain saturated fat. Vegetable oil, which has neither, is a more healthful choice, and it can be used successfully in baked goods whose texture doesn't depend on creaming solid fat together with sugar.*

2. **Making the topping:** Stir the walnuts, brown sugar and the 2 teaspoons cinnamon in a small bowl until blended. Add the 2 tablespoons oil and stir with a fork until blended. Set aside.

3. **Making the cake:** Stir the flour, baking powder, baking soda, the 1 teaspoon cinnamon and the salt together in a large bowl. In a smaller bowl, combine the yogurt, the ⅓ cup oil, honey, egg and vanilla; whisk until very well blended.

4. Pour the liquid mixture over the flour mixture. Stir gently to combine. Spread two-thirds of the batter in the prepared cake pan. Sprinkle with one-third of the crumb mixture. Drop spoonfuls of the remaining batter evenly over the crumb layer and gently smooth the top. Sprinkle the remaining crumb mixture on top.

5. Bake until the top is browned and the sides begin to pull away from the pan, about 30 minutes. Transfer to a wire rack and cool before cutting into wedges and serving.

384 CALORIES PER SERVING

7 G PROTEIN

18 G FAT

49 G CARBOHYDRATE

351 MG SODIUM

28 MG CHOLESTEROL

LEMON & PEAR CRISP

Makes 6 servings

❋ *As a variation, you can add 2
tablespoons of raisins or dried
cranberries in place of the
crystallized ginger. (Crystallized
ginger, also called candied ginger,
which has been cooked in sugar
syrup and covered with sugar, is
found in the spice section of most
supermarkets.)*

❋ *You can also mix
½ teaspoon grated orange or
lemon zest with the pears.*

ATMEAL CONTRIBUTES a nutty flavor and crunchy texture, while crystallized ginger adds a distinctive bite to the fruit, keeping our palates busy with its bursts of flavor. This dessert is also good for breakfast with plain or vanilla yogurt.

4 large pears, medium-ripe, peeled, cored and quartered,
   cut into thin wedges
1 tablespoon fresh lemon juice
1 tablespoon sugar
1 tablespoon slivered crystallized ginger

Topping
½ cup quick-cooking (not instant) oatmeal
¼ cup packed light brown sugar
2 tablespoons all-purpose flour
1 tablespoon finely chopped walnuts
2 tablespoons butter, at room temperature, cut into small pieces

Vanilla ice cream or frozen yogurt (optional)

1. Preheat oven to 350 degrees F. Slice the pears into a 9- or 10-inch pie plate or other shallow baking dish. Add the lemon juice and sugar and toss just to blend. Spread evenly in the dish and sprinkle with the crystallized ginger.

2. **Making the topping:** In a medium bowl, stir together the oatmeal, brown sugar, flour and walnuts. Add the butter and work it into the mixture with a fork or your fingertips until the mixture is blended. Squeeze the mixture in your hands so that small balls form. Distribute the mixture evenly over the pears.

3. Bake until the top is browned, about 35 minutes. Serve warm or at room temperature. Top with vanilla ice cream or frozen yogurt, if desired.

185 CALORIES PER SERVING

2 G PROTEIN

5 G FAT

35 G CARBOHYDRATE

42 MG SODIUM

10 MG CHOLESTEROL

GOLDEN DELICIOUS UPSIDE-DOWN CAKE

Makes 8 servings

300 CALORIES PER SERVING

4 G PROTEIN

10 G FAT

49 G CARBOHYDRATE

338 MG SODIUM

27 MG CHOLESTEROL

THIS APPEALING CAKE is a cross between the American pineapple upside-down cake and the classic French "upside-down tart" called Tarte Tatin. Instead of butter, this cake uses low-fat milk, applesauce and vegetable oil for moisture. The apples cook in a coating of brown sugar that melts and creates a topping when the cake is inverted onto the serving plate. Dried cranberries or raisins add a festive note.

Fruit Topping

2   large Golden Delicious apples, peeled, cored and
    quartered, cut into thin wedges (about 3½ cups)

⅓   cup packed light brown sugar

2   tablespoons dried cranberries or raisins

2   tablespoons fresh lemon juice

Cake

1¾ cups all-purpose flour

¼   cup sugar

2   teaspoons baking powder

1   teaspoon baking soda

1   teaspoon ground cinnamon

½   teaspoon salt

½   cup low-fat milk

⅔   cup unsweetened applesauce

⅓   cup vegetable oil

1   large egg, beaten

1   teaspoon vanilla extract

1. Preheat oven to 350 degrees F.

2. **Making the topping:** Combine the apples, brown sugar, dried cranberries or raisins and lemon juice. Spoon into a round 9-×-3-inch cake pan (You can also use a loose-bottomed springform pan.) Spread in an even layer. Set aside.

3. **Making the cake:** Stir the flour, sugar, baking powder, baking soda, cinnamon and salt together in a large bowl. In a separate bowl, stir the milk, applesauce, oil, egg and vanilla together until blended. Pour the wet ingredients over the dry ingredients and gently stir just until blended; do not overmix. Spread the batter evenly on top of the fruit layer.

4. Bake until the cake is golden brown on top and the edges have pulled away from the sides of the pan, about 40 minutes. Cool 20 minutes on a wire rack. Loosen the sides of the cake with the tip of a small knife and invert the cake onto a serving platter. Serve warm.

CHOCOLATE HAZELNUT CAKE *with* RASPBERRY GLAZE

Makes 12 servings

THIS IS AN ELEGANT VERSION of a rich single-layer chocolate cake. It is made with vegetable oil rather than butter and with unsweetened cocoa powder, which adds a deep chocolate flavor with far less fat than in squares of chocolate. Glaze the cake with a thin film of melted raspberry jam and garnish with a few whole raspberries and some chopped toasted hazelnuts.

1	cup plus 12 whole hazelnuts
¾	cup plus 1 tablespoon sugar
	Oil and flour for pan
2	large eggs
2	egg whites
¾	cup mild-flavored vegetable oil
¼	cup strong brewed espresso coffee, at room temperature
1	teaspoon vanilla extract
¾	cup all-purpose flour
½	cup unsweetened cocoa powder
1	teaspoon baking powder
	Pinch of salt
¼	cup seedless raspberry jam
	Whole raspberries for garnish (optional)

1. Preheat oven to 350 degrees F. Spread the hazelnuts on a baking pan and heat until the skins are cracked and the nuts are toasted, about 13 minutes. Transfer to a wire mesh strainer and, protecting your hand with a potholder and holding the strainer over a bowl or the sink, rub the nuts briskly to remove the loose skins. Cool.

2. Set aside 12 hazelnuts; coarsely chop and reserve for the garnish. Finely chop the remaining hazelnuts in a food processor with 1 tablespoon of the sugar; set aside.

3. Lightly oil and flour a 10-inch springform pan; shake out the excess flour.

4. Beat the whole eggs and egg whites in a large mixing bowl until frothy. Gradually beat in the remaining ¾ cup sugar; continue beating until the mixture is pale yellow in color, about 5 minutes. At the lowest speed, beat in the oil in a slow, steady stream. Add the coffee and the vanilla.

5. Stir the flour, cocoa, baking powder and salt together in a large bowl; stir in the finely chopped toasted hazelnut-sugar mixture. Add the egg mixture and gently fold until thoroughly blended. Pour into the prepared pan.

6. Bake until the edges pull away from the sides of the pan and the center is firm to the touch, about 35 minutes. Cool on a wire rack 30 minutes. In a small saucepan, stir the raspberry jam over low heat until melted and smooth. Spread in a smooth, even layer on the top of the cake. Let stand until the cake is thoroughly cooled and the jam is set.

7. Loosen the sides of the cake with a small spatula. Remove the sides of the pan. Slide the cake onto a serving platter. Decorate the top with a border of the reserved chopped hazelnuts and evenly spaced whole raspberries, if desired. Serve in thin wedges.

281 CALORIES PER SERVING
5 G PROTEIN
21 G FAT
23 G CARBOHYDRATE
73 MG SODIUM
36 MG CHOLESTEROL

TIPS

❋ *For a different dessert, make the lemon filling separately and fill small tart shells with it. Top with fresh fruit.*

❋ *See the note on eggs, page 249.*

LEMON SPONGE CAKE
with LEMON FILLING
& STRAWBERRIES

Makes 8 to 10 servings

A SPONGE CAKE IS MADE ENTIRELY without butter, instead using egg yolks for tenderness and stiffly beaten egg whites for lightness. Twice as many whites as yolks cut the cholesterol of this cake in half. In place of some of the missing egg yolk, I add some vegetable oil to keep the cake tender. The filling, often called lemon curd, is thickened primarily with cornstarch rather than the traditional eggs and butter. The cake is lovely served plain with extra sliced strawberries on the side. Or serve with Raspberry & Strawberry Sauce (page 256) or Vanilla Custard Sauce (page 257), ladling some around each serving.

Lemon Filling

2	tablespoons cornstarch
⅓	cup sugar
½	cup apple juice
½	cup fresh lemon juice
2	egg yolks, lightly beaten
2	teaspoons grated lemon zest
1	tablespoon butter

Lemon Sponge Cake

Vegetable-oil cooking spray
Flour for pan

3	large eggs, separated
3	egg whites
¼	teaspoon salt
6	tablespoons sugar

1   tablespoon vegetable oil
1   teaspoon vanilla extract
1½ teaspoons grated lemon zest
6   tablespoons cornstarch
6   tablespoons all-purpose flour
1   pint strawberries, sliced
    (reserve 3 whole berries for garnish)

1   tablespoon confectioners' sugar

221 CALORIES PER SERVING

5 G PROTEIN

7 G FAT

36 G CARBOHYDRATE

129 MG SODIUM

137 MG CHOLESTEROL

1. **Making the filling:** In a medium saucepan, stir the cornstarch and sugar until blended. Gradually add the juices, stirring, until smooth. Stir in the egg yolks and zest.

2. Cook the mixture over medium heat, stirring constantly, until very thick. Remove from heat and stir in the butter. Pour the mixture into a bowl and cover with wax paper so that the paper rests on the surface of the filling. Refrigerate until cool.

3. **Meanwhile, make the cake:** Preheat oven to 400 degrees F. Spray the surface of a 15-x-10-inch jelly roll pan with vegetable-oil cooking spray. Line with a sheet of wax paper; spray again. Sprinkle lightly with flour and shake off the excess.

4. Beat the 6 egg whites and salt on medium speed with an electric mixer until soft peaks form. Gradually beat in the sugar, 1 tablespoon at a time; continue to beat until the whites are shiny, about 5 minutes.

5. Whisk the egg yolks, oil, vanilla and zest in a bowl. Stir in a spoonful of the whites until blended. Pour the yolk mixture over the whites. Sift the cornstarch and flour into the bowl of the whites and yolks and fold them all together gently, but thoroughly. Do not overmix.

6. Spread the batter evenly in the prepared pan and bake until barely golden, about 10 to 12 minutes. Transfer to a wire rack and immediately slide the sponge layer, wax paper side down, onto the rack. Cool 20 minutes with the wax paper on. Invert the cake and peel off the paper when cool.

7. Place the sponge layer, smooth side down, on a clean dishcloth or a piece of wax paper. Spread evenly with the cooled lemon filling to within ½ inch of the edges. Spacing the sliced strawberries evenly, arrange the berries in rows on the lemon filling.

8. Working from one of the short sides and using the dishcloth or wax paper as a guide, roll up the sponge layer. Place on a serving plate. Garnish with the whole or halved berries. Place the confectioners' sugar in a small sieve and dust the top of the sponge roll liberally. Garnish with the reserved whole strawberries.

9. Serve on a pool of Raspberry & Strawberry Sauce or Vanilla Custard Sauce.

INDEX